All
Because
Of Him

by

Klara Andersen

Illustrated by the Author

To Pauline with Best Wishes, Klara Andersen, ↓ "alias" Edel

i

First Published by Fowey Rare Books 1995
4 South Street, Fowey, Cornwall PL23 1AR

© Klara Andersen 1995

ISBN 1 899526 05 6

Printed in Great Britain by
Alexander Associates, Fowey

British Library Cataloguing in Publication Data. A catalogue record for this book
is available from the British Library.

CONTENTS

(Including 13 photographs, 12 drawings and 33 silhouettes)

FOREWORD

Ever since I came to this country in 1950 I have been asked whether the ordinary people in Germany *really* didn't know what Hitler was up to, and why no-one was able to stop him?

So I decided that one day I would write about those days, about my own family and other ordinary people. But it wasn't until I retired, after I had lived and taught in the West-Country since 1958, that I began to piece together the different episodes.

My early memories are of the time when many citizens, including my parents, would laugh at the idea of '*That Man*' coming to power! But then he *did* gain the trust of many people, and by the time the sinister side of the regime began to affect us, it was too late to stop its progress.

I used to keep a diary from the age of ten, at first only recording childish events such as the day I found a four-leafed clover....

Later on, though, I wrote of the plight of our Jewish Doctor, and of my feelings of annoyance, when it became compulsory to join the 'Young Maidens' in 1936!

However, my Grammar School teacher warned me *never* to put on paper any comments about the Nazi-Party, or air views contrary to the official version of events....

And as a result I burnt my diaries!

But that same teacher used to urge me to write, write, write, as long as it wasn't about anything to do with politics!

"ALL BECAUSE OF HIM" tells of those days, as seen through a young person's eyes. The stories are based on real events, though I've changed some of the names. And perhaps the old schoolmaster would be pleased if he were still here! I'm sure he would approve of my pen-name, which I have taken from my father's Danish mother:

She was called Mette Christine Andersen and was born in Odense on the Island of Funen, which was also the birthplace of Hans Christian Andersen. I remember a visit of our aged maiden-aunt Anna Andersen, when she told me that the famous Danish story-teller was our great-great-uncle. (I've forgotten how many 'Greats' she said!)

When I told the teacher about this, he said that writing must be in my blood!

So I should like to dedicate 'ALL BECAUSE OF HIM' to the memory of my old schoolmaster, without whose timely intervention I might have landed myself and my family in the hands of the Gestapo. There were many courageous people I came across during the years before and after the war, impossible to name them all. But one person stands out in that line of unsung heroes; and even though I never knew his name, I feel he ought to be remembered:

The old man who risked his life helping me and my companions to escape to the free West in 1948.

St. Austell. November 1994   Klara Andersen

"...and all because of HIM..."

Piano Lessons

IT was in the late summer of 1932. I was eight years old, and I didn't want to have piano lessons! I hated the idea!

But the odds were against me: Mother was a domineering woman; and I was sure that my father would agree for the sake of peace and quiet—what else could he do, faced by the combined efforts of two determined females such as my mother and my teacher?

It all started when the schoolmarm arrived for one of her periodical visits.

Waiting on our doorstep, she must have recognized the tune coming from a piano somewhere inside the flat. It was played with just one finger, but it WAS the song she had been teaching her class earlier that day:

All about billowing flags and the dawn of freedom....

I did not understand the meaning of it, but I liked the melody. And because I could not sing a single note when I was little, I used to turn to the piano to recapture a tune.

And now the teacher wanted to know who was playing.

When she was told, she brushed past Mother and rushed into the sitting room to see for herself!

I had only just managed to slip off the piano stool. Hearing her strident voice, I had wanted to hide. But it was too late!

"Who would have guessed it," she declared, "you were playing perfectly in tune!"

I couldn't think of a reply, and she added:

All Because Of Him

"And I always thought you had no ear at all!"

Whatever did she mean ? Of course I had — two of them ! And how rude she was, to push past Mother like that!

She was always telling us to mind our manners in class! But adults were like that...they said one thing and meant another! Mother was just the same: I knew she didn't really like the teacher, and yet she was fussing over her as if she was an honoured guest !

Still, in Mother's book people such as teachers, vicars, doctors and the local chemist all belonged to what she used to call "our circles". I don't think she ever faced up to the fact that she had left those realms when she married Father, who was a clerk in an ordinary office.

Now she said she'd make some coffee, and before leaving the room she turned to me:

"Sit on your chair, and talk to your teacher nicely!"

As if I'd dare to open my mouth, unless I was spoken to first! I sat down, feeling the woman's gaze resting on me — and when she'd finished eyeing me, she began a survey of the room.

First she looked at the family photographs...then she pinched the soil in Mother's plant pots, like testing if they were over or under-watered — and when she reached the sideboard with our Russian Samovar, she wagged her head from side to side. I thought perhaps she didn't hold with foreign customs. I was watching her move from place to place.

Whenever I looked at her in school or at home, she gave me the impression of something vast and grey: Wispy bits of grey hair were sticking out from the bun on the back of her head, twitching like a cat's whiskers, as she wagged and nodded in turn.

She always wore a grey dress, which was bulging at the top like a ship's prow — a sort of Spanish Galleon in human form.

To the children in her class she could be awe-inspiring!

But I was certain that Mother was not in awe of her. And the fact that the woman had turned out to be a fanatical admirer of Hitler did not intimidate her in the least!

But it was early days yet....

Before her visits no-one had mentioned the name of Hitler or his Party in front of us children. She called him her HERO. But we were too young to understand her idolatry of the man.

And my mother always referred to him contemptiously as 'that man

Hitler' ! Yet the woman would not be put off and would always manage to bring the conversation around to Politics.

Even now, as she wandered about in our sitting room, she started on the subject:

"I see your parents still haven't got a picture of Hitler anywhere! What a pity your mother is so opposed to his ideas!"

I didn't think she expected me to answer. So I just nodded, and she continued her inspection.

Our family lived quietly in a quiet suburb of Hanover, and neither of my parents had any firm political leanings.

My father was a quiet, peace-loving man. He had to spend all day in a stuffy office. And he often brought home a briefcase full of files, working till late at night to correct some error. Business records were still written by hand and entered into enormous folios during his working life.

So his few hours of freedom were precious to him; but above all, it would have been out of character for him to attend rowdy party-meetings or rallies.

As for Mother: I knew that she still dreamed of the old days, when they had the Kaiser — I thought it must have something to do with her cherished 'Circles'!

Both my parents would have dismissed the idea of Hitler coming to power. Like many other people in Germany at that time, they didn't really believe his rantings needed to be taken seriously. But then: most people in Germany hadn't read his book !

At last Mother appeared with coffee and biscuits, and from that moment onwards, the two of them completely ignored me.

I didn't mind. It was always the same when we had visitors.

At first they talked about school and homework, and how well I was doing. But then the conversation switched to my one-finger-exercise at the piano, and I pricked up my ears.

"I think the child should have lessons," the teacher said. "It is pointless tinkering about as she does. I should like to teach her to play properly."

This was unexpected, and unwanted, as far as I was concerned !

But she was very persuasive, and when she noticed that my mother hesitated, she added as an extra bait:

"Of course, if she's up to a certain standard by the time of the school concert, she can take part !"

3

All Because Of Him

I was listening with baited breath, terrified in case Mother agreed. This promise about the school concert might prove irresistible.

Even in those early years she was probably aware that she favoured my younger sister, though no power on earth could make her admit it. And with her strict Christian background she must have felt guilty about this lack of affection.

So she used to make a big thing of my achievements as a sort of compensation—but there were times, when I would have loved to be hugged rather than praised !

Sitting quietly, legs tucked under, hands clasped in my lap, I was praying that the teacher's offer would be refused! Wasn't it bad enough to endure her in class! The thought of being the sole focus of her attention for a whole hour was appalling !

I could picture myself on the piano stool, with her squatting close to me: there would not be enough space between us to avoid the spittle that used to spurt from her mouth whenever she became excited or irritable (it used to fascinate us kids during lessons, as long as we were not near enough to be in the firing line!)

Mother said that we couldn't afford any extra expenses... but before I could breathe a sigh of relief, Teacher assured her that there would be no fees, that it would be a pleasure to teach me !

After that Mother promised to discuss it with her husband. She would send a note to let her know by to-morrow.

Thereafter they talked about other topics.

I let it all wash over me, torn between the prospect of the lessons and the faint hope that my father might not agree to their scheme!

After a while the teacher got around to Politics.

As always when she was talking about HIM, she got more and more excited; and she soon reached the sputtering stage: Drops were flying all over the biscuits my mother had placed in front of her. I decided not to have any more biscuits until that tin had been emptied!

Mother maintained she didn't think that Hitler's coming to power would bring Germany a glorious future!

"But my dear," Teacher assured her, "he will lead us all out of the pit !"

"Here she goes again !" I thought. "What is she talking about?"

I knew we weren't well off, but neither my family nor any of our friends were living in a pit ! Anyway, according to Mother 'this man Hitler' could be no good, because he didn't believe in God! She said:

"He's always referring to 'Providence', so he *must* be an Atheist!"

She'd been born in 1894 and had been brought up in a strict Protestant household. Her father had been a vicar...so she knew all the answers!

But I wondered what an Atheist was?

At one stage the teacher sighed and said wistfully:

"If only I were younger, I should love to have a child by him!"

Of course, due to my blinkered upbringing, I had no idea what she meant. But their ensuing talk about birth sort of stuck in my mind. (I tried to find the words in Father's Encyclopedia afterwards, but Mother had taped the relevant pages together to keep me in ignorance!)

Time ticked on. Through the open window, I could hear the voices of my playmates — they seemed to be having a great time in our camp on the allotment, while I was stuck indoors! And I wished the woman were miles away: She *and* her man Hitler!

At long last she rose to go.

As soon as the door had closed behind her, I ran out onto the balcony to watch for Father's return. I wanted to catch him before Mother could broach the subject of the lessons.

But he arrived late that evening, carrying a large folder to work on after supper. So we all sat down to our meal as soon as he had changed into his rumpled old housecoat.

He looked warm and loveable, sitting opposite me at the table. I yearned to speak to him alone!

But Jutta came in and clambered onto her chair. Then Mother carried in the soup, and while she was serving, she started reporting the day's events....

And the subject of the piano lessons came up almost at once.

I tried to signal across the table, hoping Father could read the message in my eyes. But he was looking at *her*.

She seemed determined to make him see all the advantages! By the time she was talking about the school concert, I had become so desperate, I did an un-heard-of thing:

I interrupted while she was speaking!

"Please don't make me have those lessons!"

Father turned to me. His kind face was full of concern. I looked straight at him, sort of willing him him to help me out of the music-trap!

But before he could say anything, Mother cut short any argument by telling me to eat my supper, adding:

"You know children don't talk at the table!"

Oh, what was the use!

How could I eat, feeling all chokèd up and full of misery! My mouth was dry and my eyes wanted to overflow.

But she mustn't see that I was about to cry!

Father had noticed it, though, and gave me a quick, reassuring smile. But he waited till Mother had finished talking about the golden opportunity, before saying his piece.

"I suppose your teacher meant well." He said. "Shall we try it for, say, three or four months and see how you get on?"

I didn't want to try it for even one session. But I didn't dare to explain about the spittle, or my dislike of the woman. So I only nodded, keeping my eyes down, because the tears were still threatening to well up. He said:

"Now, now, little Tramp, don't cry! I promise, if you want to stop after that time, we'll call it a day! Free tuition or not!"

Oh, how I loved him! Whenever he called me his 'little Tramp', it meant he was on my side! And he'd managed to let me see a way out without getting Mother all vexed!

I wanted to get off my chair and hug him. But the meal wasn't finished yet and Mother would scold me, would say that it wasn't done....

Still, I had his promise! I could eat without choking!

By now Jutta, who had just got over Measles, was sitting limply on her chair, and Mother decided to put her to bed.

When she returned to the table, I noticed the 'That's-settled-then' look on her face. I knew she felt she'd scored a point about the lessons!

Then they went on dicussing the teacher; and I heard her say:

"You know, she's very knowledgable but not much to look at!"

"Why?"

"Oh, she's fat. Her hair's screwed into a wispy bun, her dress is ill-fitting, with a dipping hem... and she wears *men's* shoes!"

It made my father chuckle, and she went on:

"And she's got legs like champagne-bottles!"

Now they both laughed.

I, too, was overcome by a desire to giggle, but I didn't want to remind them of my presence, because I'd be sent straight to bed.

I made a mental note, though: first thing in school tomorrow, I would have a look at the teacher's lower half to see about those legs!

Next morning I delivered Mother's note to the teacher.

After a quick glance at it, she nodded and said:

"Good. You can start on Monday after school. And don't dawdle on the way! My time is very precious!"

As she climbed onto the platform to start the lesson, I thought rebelliously, that I hadn't asked for her precious time in the first place! And I remembered to look at her legs only just before they disappeared behind her desk:

Mother was right! They did look like bottles: Thin at the ankles and then bulging out by the calves in a sort of over-full curve.

Monday came, too soon for me; and I walked the half mile up our road to her flat. I climbed the stairs and rang the bell. The door was opened by a woman who stared at me as if I were a beggar asking for a crust. I knew she must be the housekeeper.

She seemed dressed to go out, and when she'd finished staring, she said:

"Miss says you are to wait here till she's finished her coffee. Now don't touch anything!"

Then she swept past me and out of the flat, while I stood there, hardly daring to breathe, leave alone touch anything.

After what seemed ages, the teacher appeared from behind one of the doors leading out of the hall. She gave a quick nod and told me to follow her into the music room. But before I'd got over the threshold, she put a restraining hand on my arm:

"Mind you don't step on the floor! Just go from one mat to the other, till you get to the piano. I don't want marks on the lino!"

Oh Lord!

The room seemed vast, more than twice the size of our sitting room! And there were numerous small, oval rush mats placed like stepping stones on the shiniest lino I had ever seen — it was shinier than the inlaid floor in King George the First's castle, down by the river Leine! She had taken us there on a school outing, and we had all been given huge felt slippers to shuffle about in.

I thought of those slippers, as I stood there, terrified in case I couldn't make the distance between the mats! They were like islands in an ocean, spaced much too far apart for my short legs! And once I started to jump, the beastly things tended to slip forward on landing — so my arms were flailing

All Because Of Him

like windmills to keep my balance.

Of course, *she* had arrived at the piano well before me and was watching my progress. Every time I missed my footing she shook her head and demanded I should be more careful!

When I reached the piano stool at last, my relief was short lived: I discovered that it was one of those double seats, made for two people to play together! Oh! She would be so close to me! How could I duck away from the sputterings!

However, we were soon installed side by side on the scratchy red plush of the seat; and she lost no time before starting on my first finger exercises. I lost count of the endless scales to which she kept nodding her head in rhythmic motion... her face hovering above my left shoulder... far too close for comfort!

No student of any music lesson has ever been more relieved, when the hour was up! Of course, before I could escape, the stepping stone ritual had to be repeated in reverse order — When I reached the door, she patted my head and said:

"Well done!"

I wasn't sure whether she meant my efforts at the piano or the leaps between the mats....

Later that evening, when I went to kiss my father good-night, he wanted to know how the lesson had gone. My mother was out of the room at the time, putting Jutta to bed.

"Was it very difficult?" He asked.

"No-o, but I didn't like the jumping!"

He looked mystified, and when I explained, he laughed, until I protested:

"It wasn't funny at the time! All that hopping about!"

He said that he hadn't been laughing at *me*.

"It was just the thought of your fussy school mistress and her precious lino!"

"Do I have to go again?" I asked. It was half question and half plea.

He hesitated before replying. Maybe he was trying to figure out a way to overcome my disappointment. Then he said:

"Try to keep at it! It's good to learn perseverance!"

He saw the puzzled look on my face and went on:

"When we grow up, things often don't turn out as we'd hoped. Then we have to persevere and make the best of what we've got."

It was quite a sermon, at least for my father. And I remembered his words, even though I didn't grasp their meaning until many years later. At the time, I only knew that I wanted to please him.

So I agreed to go on with the weekly trip to the teacher's flat.

Several months later she decided that I should be included in the concert. It was to take place in the summer term, and when she told me of it, I thought of Dad's words and promised to do my best.

She said she would be proud of me, if I did well!

I had by now more or less mastered the distance between the mats. Maybe I had become less clumsy...or perhaps my legs had grown since I started the lessons — so things weren't too bad that way.

If only I didn't have to be so close to her on that piano stool! It didn't matter whether I did well with the scales, or whether I made her vexed with a faulty finger position, sooner or later she always got to the spittle stage! And that was the worst of it!

On the occasions when I'd done well, she would reward me with a delicious piece of fruit cake, baked by the housekeeper.

But the fuss she made about the crumbs I might drop, and even about the way I should hold the cake made me think I'd rather do without....

"Spread your skirt, child! Put your left hand beneath your right one, so nothing can fall on the floor!"

Sitting on one of her stiff, uncomfortable best chairs, I hardly dared to take a proper bite.

She would be enthroned on the sofa opposite me, eyeing my lips; and to avoid staring at her, I used to look at the many photographs gazing at me from around the room.

There was a large one of a man in uniform.

He had a small moustache, and he wore a sort of band around his left arm with a strange symbol on it. I had seen similar designs on pictures of ancient Greek vases in one of Father's books.

I thought it was funny to have that on his sleeve!

She noticed my interest and said:

"That is Hitler. He's a great man. He'll make Germany into a proud nation again!"

"So this is the Atheist!" I thought and studied the man's face. There was nothing special to his features, as far as I could make out. His eyes were

....his eyes were rather stary — they seemed to follow you
if you changed position...

rather stary — they seemed to follow you if you changed position.

I noticed this one day, when I went to the coal scuttle to shake off the crumbs. Watching the Atheist's eyes, I forgot to watch the way I held up my skirt, and she gasped:

"Look out! Hold on to your skirt! Or you'll make a mess!"

After that, I paid no more attention to the man with the armband. It was more important to reach the coal scuttle without losing a crumb or missing the mats....

Then in January 1933 Hitler came to power.

And from then on there were no bounds to the teacher's hero worship!

She hung up a life sized photo of him in the classroom. From there he was fixing us with his stare throughout each lesson; and if we got tired of his constant gaze and turned our eyes to the windows, we were accused of not paying attention!

Summer came. The time of the concert was approaching... and about a fortnight before the great day, I fell and had to have my right arm in plaster! So my name had to be crossed off the programme....

Teacher must have been annoyed about it, because she took a kind of subtle revenge on me for being so clumsy! She cleverly disguised it though, even tried to make it look like a compliment:

A few days after I'd had the fall, she called me to her desk and handed me a postcard with a photo of Hitler's chalet in the Bavarian Alps.

"Here you are," she said, "you can do a big picture of it on the black-board!"

And she pointed to the big rectangular blackboard, extending almost along one entire wall....

I looked at her helplessly; and, not knowing how to protest, I lifted my bandaged arm up to her. She looked at it coldly:

"So what?"

I said meekly:

"I can't with this on!"

"Nonsense, child! You can draw so well, you can do it with your left hand!"

And she handed me a new box of coloured chalks for the job.

Hesitatingly, I approached the blackboard.

But she told me to wait:

"Here, climb onto the stool, then you can reach right up to the top and do the mountains as well!"

The stool was as high as a normal chair, but she never even helped me climb onto it! It was a wobbly old thing, normally reserved for miscreants to sit in a corner—a throne of shame as it were.

I managed to draw a passable picture, even though I had to adjust the hick-hocking of the stool to the movements of my left arm, and even though, every time I'd got to the end of my reach, I'd had to climb off, shift the seat further along, and then climb up again....

All the while, her voice was droning away at the back of me, extolling the virtues of Hitler, telling the class that the chalet was where he went to have a rest from ruling the country!

When I'd finished, she praised my efforts effusively, but I was angry because of the ordeal she'd put me through. And when I explained to Mother, how the chalk had got on my clothes as well as on the plaster, she was angry too! Very angry!

She told Father about it during supper. And they both agreed without argument: No more piano lessons!

However, Dad being Dad, it was decided not to mention this to the teacher at present, as we were close to the end of term anyway.

My moment of triumph came after the holidays, when I returned to school without the plaster:

Teacher looked at my arm and said I should resume the piano lessons next Monday!

Then I slowly rose from my chair, walked up to her desk and handed her a note from my father:

She said nothing, only just nodded her head so the bits of wispy hair were all a-trembling, and then she gave me one of her piercing angry stares—

And that was the end of my musical career.

Disenchantment

SUMMER 1933. Our teacher was in her element! The unthinkable had happened: Hitler had come to power in January, and since then not a day had gone by without her singing his praises to the nine-yearold girls in her class. She would have liked to transform the classroom into a shrine, but to begin with she contented herself by hanging up her idol's lifesize portrait above her desk. From there he was staring at us with his hypnotic gaze. I was sure his eyes followed us around the room....

She then proceeded to scan the newspapers for announcements of the whereabouts of her beloved. And if there was a chance to get a glimpse of him on his way to or from Hanover airport, or outside one of the hotels or the town hall, she would drag a chosen selection of well behaved pupils all over the place to stand by the roadside and present him with flowers.

Even if it was pouring with rain, she wouldn't be deterred!

I remember one such outing, about a week before the end of the summer term.

We were waiting on the approach road to the airport. The water began to trickle down inside my mac, my shoes were full of it, and my resentment of the fanatical teacher grew by the minute.

She kept on saying we mustn't be discouraged!

"Just think how happy the Fuehrer will be to see you, waiting for him in spite of the rain!"

After she had told us for the umpteenth time that he would be here soon; a man came out from the big swing doors of the airport lounge and announced that Hitler had had to change his plans. Instead of him the Culture-and-Propaganda Minister Joseph Goebbels would be arriving shortly.

So she decided that we would wait for Goebbels and give him our flowers.... the flowers, which she provided on these outings, were by now looking as bedraggled as the children.

And we waited.

We waited for over two hours, and then the man came out again to say that due to the weather the plane had been diverted!

So we got back onto the tram, dripping like drowned rats, and a few of us didn't turn up in school the next day.

Teacher had several notes on her desk, all sent by incensed mothers, whose daughters had got the sniffles; but I don't think it worried *her* ! That sort of complaint was brushed aside....

The only child in my class who was always excluded from any of these outings was a girl called Ellie. Teacher never had her on her list of chosen girls, because she had been crippled by Polio and walked with a bad limp. She lived in the flat above us, and I used to help her on the way to and from school, acting as a sort of living crutch... and I often wondered how she must feel, always being left out of things!

But a few days after our washed-out trip to the airport, she told me that, for once, she was glad she hadn't been able to come.

"At least I didn't have to get half-drowned just to please our silly old teacher!"

Hobbling along beside me on the way to our play area, she stuck her freckled nose up in the air and added:

"My mum says it's wrong to worship people, anyway!"

I nodded. I knew that both our mothers didn't like the Fuehrer, but that they had come to the conclusion that there was nothing anyone could do about it, because he was now in charge of the country.

We would have to wait and see.

I told her how I'd heard the teacher say to my Mother that Hitler would 'lead us all out of the pit'! But that I couldn't make sense of such strange grown-up talk....

"I wish people wouldn't talk in riddles!" She sighed, and then she changed the subject:

"You know what? Martin says he wants to join the Hitler Youth! But I don't think my father will let him! Are you going to join?"

Disenchantment

"No, I wanted to , but my parents said'no'."

I admitted to being tempted; but what had attracted me was merely the uniform: I thought I should look smart in it!

In my family there never seemed to be enough money for really nice new clothes. Jutta and I often had to make do with hand-me- downs from Mother's relatives. Twice a year our home dressmaker would arrive with her book of patterns and her big scissors. She would attempt to transform some faded old frocks from the cousins into faded new ones for Jutta and me.

Mother had told the seamstress of my wish to join the Hitler-Youth, and they had both laughed at the idea....

And the dressmaker had said that she wouldn't be allowed to make the uniform, because it had to be bought from some special Department. Mother had declared that we couldn't afford it, in any case; and that had been the end of it!

(In the years to come I was glad my parents had refused to budge on that issue, and had held out against my joining the Hitler Youth until it became compulsory in December 1936.)

Anyway, my desire to look smart had soon been forgotten; and I now told Ellie that she and I were much better off just being members of our own gang, instead of having to march through the streets, shouting battle hymns!

"We'd miss our games with the others," I said, "especially in the summer!"

"And Bernie and Jo would miss US!" She said and I agreed.

We mustn't be disloyal to our gang-leaders!

By now we had reached the end of the cul-de-sac.

There was a wilderness of abandoned allotments, waiting to be built on...and this was our play-area....

We had all congregated there ever since we'd moved into the new blocks of flats. Boys and girls between the ages of eight and twelve, including Ellie and myself, belonged to what we proudly called the 'Gang'... and the allotments were our own undisputed domain!

During the holidays we usually split up into two teams, and then we often fought battles with pellets made from clay. (We'd discovered the clay, when we were digging the camps; and Bernie had at once recognized its potential for use as ammunition!)

The shallow pits we had dug had served in turn as log-cabins, hospitals, tepees, or whatever the occasion demanded....

On wet days we would sit under a ragged piece of roof that had been blown off some discarded garden shed. Huddled together, we used to listen to the stories from Bernie's comics, taking turns at reading aloud....

So far, we'd lived happily in our pretend-realm.

Events from the troubled real world had not yet begun to intrude....

"Only one more day!" Ellie said as I was helping her pick her way through the maze of dying undergrowth and rotten fencing to get to our dug-out. Some of the other children were already sitting around the edge of the camp, listening to Bernie.

When we got close enough, we could hear that he seemed to be outlining the strategy for our next campaign!

"We'll be on holiday after tomorrow; so we'll do it Saturday if the weather's fine!"

"Roll on Saturday!" Ellie said, and they all cheered.

After we'd had a good pow-wow about the planned battle, we went back to our respective homes. I think at that time most of us were still eager and happy, still looking forward to the weeks of unfettered freedom, still sure of the sun smiling down on us, sure that nothing was going to change....

There would be only Thursday to struggle through, and then we wouldn't have to see the schoolmarm for ages! She could worship the Fuehrer without dragging US along every time !

But when we had said our compulsory 'Heil Hitler' at the start of Thursday's lessons, the teacher announced that there was to be a big rally in the Stadium this Saturday, attended by the Fuehrer!

She would take a selected number of us to line the road, and she herself would provide the flowers we were to give him!

Saturday! Had she forgotten we would be on holiday by then?

No, she hadn't. She said:

"I have written to the parents concerned and have asked them to come along as well, so they can take you home afterwards!"

And she reeled off the names....

As expected, I was one of the 'Chosen Ones'.

When my parents got the letter, Mother said that she had no wish to stand shouting and waving by the wayside. But our true and trusting father said he wouldn't mind having a look at Hitler, because he had never seen him in person.

Disenchantment

In the days before Television, people had to rely mostly on poor quality photos in the press, unless they went to the Cinema. And in our family Cinemas were only just one shade better than gaming houses, (according to Mother!).

To persuade her to come, my father suggested we might all go to the Zoo after the spectacle was over.

It seemed a lovely idea! I thought it would make up for missing the battle with Bernie and the others.

My sister Jutta, just five years old, was hopping about with glee at the prospect of seeing all the animals.

But then Mother told her that she was too small to be taken among crowds all shouting and waving, and Julia looked crestfallen...till Father said soothingly:

"Surely the SS-Men lining the roads will let a little one like her slip in front of them!"

Mother bristled at his 'ill-founded trust', as she called it!

Everyone knew that the SS were Hitler's Elite-Guards. But some people also suspected that they had not only been chosen for their blond Aryan looks, but for their capacity to be ruthless and brutal!

So she said in her 'You-mark-my-words' kind of voice:

"I don't think those men *would* make an exception! They are a vicious lot. I have heard terrible rumours of rough justice! Absolutely hair-raising, I tell you!"

Father cleared his throat. It meant that he didn't agree, but he didn't want to have an argument with his wife. Being such an honest, peace-loving person, he found it hard to think or speak ill of anyone. In the end it was decided we should go.

I had to tell Bernie that he would have to do without my aid during the great Saturday campaign.

But to my surprise, he was not at all put out. He said he was pleased for me, and that it was an honour to be chosen to present flowers to the Fuehrer!

I couldn't believe it!

Was this my old friend Bernie talking?

Since when had *he* become interested in the affairs of State?

I explained that I wasn't going to be the only one there, that Teacher was going to take a selection of girls, and I added:

"In any case, if his car is going too fast, we won't be able to give him our flowers! It will all be a waste of time! I'd much rather be with you and the gang!"

He drew himself up to his full height (half a head taller than his ignorant play-mate).

"Maybe you just aren't old enough to understand politics!"

He sounded so different from the boy I'd known and admired for years, especially when he declared:

"Next month I'll be twelve! Then I'll join the Hitler Youth! I dare say I shan't have much time for games after that!"

Ping! Went one of my heart strings! Bernie had been the leader of our little band from the very beginning. I had looked up to him as a hero and special protector! This would have an effect on each one of us, on our friendship, on everything!

Of course, if I'd been just a little older, a little wiser, his haughty statement might not have come as such a shock! Everybody in the street knew that his father was a keen supporter of the new Regime.

And there was something else his childish boast had made plain: for the first time since we'd played together, I became aware of the gap in our ages. Almost three years! It hadn't seemed to matter until now.... I sank my head and turned away to go home. But he put his hand on my arm and said:

"Never mind, we'll have lots more battles before the holidays are over!"

Neither of us could have known it:

He had uttered a prophesy as far as our happy times with the gang were concerned....

Saturday morning came, and Mother was pressing our clean dresses for the outing. Father had taken the morning off from the office, and when we'd packed the picnic basket, we set out on the tram ride to get to the appointed place.

The teacher was already there. We spotted her as soon as we got off the tram. Some of the other girls from my class stood in a bunch close to her. She herself was in deep conversation with one of the SS Officers. The SS men were all in position, even though Hitler was not expected for at least another hour.

She looked up, noticed my family and beckoned us to join her, and when we'd got close enough, she stuck out her ample bosom and declared proudly:

"I have just been talking to this kind SS Officer, and he has given permission for my girls to stand in front of the Guards, so they can give their flowers to the Fuehrer!"

There was a basket by her feet, filled with several bunches of flowers, all slightly the worse for wear....

I thought wickedly:

"I bet she's got them cheap, because they'll be too old to sell after the week-end!"

She now pointed to a space further up the road, saying:

"That's where we shall be in the best position! Come along now everybody, before the crowds get any larger!"

With that she began to herd us along the road. The stones at our feet seemed to reflect a violent heat already, even though it was only just past midday....

The parents followed behind, somewhat diffidently.

I wondered if some of them were like my own parents: One decidedly anti-Hitler, the other one still thinking that although there might be some wrong elements among his followers, Hitler himself surely couldn't be evil!

Believing it would all come right in the end....

Within no time at all, the chosen girls were standing in front of the men in their black uniforms, who were by now ready to link arms to hold back the crowds. The teacher had withdrawn to a space just behind their lines, from where, she hoped, she could keep an eye on us.

However, the parents and all our younger brothers and sisters had to wait jammed in among the throng, which grew ever tighter as more and more people were arriving.

Somewhere behind me, I could hear small children crying, fretting because of the sun beating down and people all around them hemming them in. I knew my parents must be somewhere behind the tall SS Man who stood at the curb next to me. I could hear them talking. And glancing to right and left, I could see my classmates holding the tired flowers in hot sticky hands. *She* had given me the roses. I had already got blood on my hanky from the thorny stems.

After a while I heard my father's quiet voice. He was trying to soothe my sister, who seemed by now well and truly stuck among all the legs... legs in front and legs behind! A whole forest of them! He wouldn't even be able to lift her up if he'd tried to!

"I can't see anything! I can't breathe!" She wailed, but then she must

...."I can see now !" she piped up....

have thought that she could find a way out of this jungle by squeezing through between the black trouser legs of the nearest SS Man....

He was standing with his feet planted apart like all the other Guards, preparing to brace themselves against the pressure from the masses behind.

And suddenly there was my little sister, with her head sticking out between his legs! She had an arm around each one, as if holding on to a tree trunk either side of her....

"I can see now!" She piped up.

But even as I turned to her, I saw the man jerk his legs, pushing her head back, calling out to the people behind him:

"Whose child is this?"

From where my father stood, he could not have seen the spiteful action. Maybe he still thought there was a chance of getting Jutta to a safe place in front. As I looked up at the SS Man's stone-cold face, I saw a hand come out from behind and tap his shoulder. It was my father's... then I heard his voice:

"Would you mind if that little girl came out in front? Next to her sister?"

But the man turned his head and snarled:

"If you DON'T KEEP her back, I'll THROW her back - right over everybody's head!"

There was a murmur from the people standing nearest. I heard Jutta crying, and someone said soothing words, apparently guiding her through the tightness to where my parents were, about two rows behind me. But before I could breathe a sigh of relief for Jutta, there was my mother's voice, and even though I couldn't see her or my father, I could picture what was going on! She kept saying:

"Don't! Calm down, don't!"

And in between there was Father's voice, in a tone I'd never heard him use before. I caught snatches of it like " viper from a snake pit" and "to think that's the ELITE!"

I prayed that Mother would manage to get him away before some terrible calamity could befall him!

At the same time I asked God not to let me get lost in the crowd once they'd gone! I was frightened, but I felt angry as well, all sort of mixed together.

After what seemed ages, I heard Mother call out from somewhere further back in the crowd, saying they would wait for me at the tram stop. And then I felt utterly alone, even though on either side of me my classmates were waiting for their big moment....

Maybe I'd better pray a little more! I thought I'd add a sort of incentive in case God was slow in coming to my aid:

"Please,God, don't let me be lost! I promise I'll go to Sunday School tomorrow with a good heart!"

(God would see that this was a difficult promise for me, because I loathed Sunday School! I was also hoping HE would notice that I'd only mentioned tomorrow, not every Sunday in the weeks to come!)

There was still no sign of Hitler's imminent arrival.

Oh, I wished I could go home! The sun was burning down with its white hot glare. My nose was full of dust,and my eyes were stinging with the tears I wouldn't allow to brim over.

For one hopeful moment I wondered if I might just be dreaming all this? A really bad dream, a nightmare? Maybe I'd had too much sun? I'd heard it could do strange things to people's heads....

But no, it was true, even though it seemed unbelievable: I knew I had not imagined or dreamt up my mother's agitated voice as she tried to calm down my father! I KNEW he had wanted to hit that SS Man!

MY FATHER!

He'd never smacked either of us girls. I'd never even seen him swat a fly!

Oh, I hated my teacher! It was all her fault. There she was, nattering away behind me. It sounded as if she was trying to make it clear to those around her that the incident had nothing to do with anyone SHE knew....

At last there was a rumble of voices, like a wave from a long way off...and as it came nearer, the people began to shout:

"He's coming! He's coming!"

And then the teacher's voice:

"Be ready girls - hold up your flowers!"

Then the shouting became as one with the wave of the far voices and there was the shiny black car: The man from the picture in the classroom had sprang to life, uniform, funny black moustache and all! The car was moving slowly... slow enough for us to step forward one by one and hold up our flowers.

He bent down to us...and his face was smiling! I thought he looked nicer than his picture, sort of friendlier, not staring or stern, and I hoped he wouldn't get hurt by the thorns on my roses! We gave him our half-dead flowers, there was a quick touch of his hand... and then he was gone.

Within seconds the crowds began to disperse. It was quite weird. The SS Men, too, re-grouped and left the scene.

And then our teacher stepped forward and said in an awestruck voice:

"Oh, you lucky girls, now you mustn't wash your hands all day, because HE has touched you!"

"No fear," I thought,"I'll be glad to get home and wash off all the sweat and stickiness!"

I'd forgotten we were going to the Zoo. Somehow I didn't feel like going anywhere but home....

Then she noticed me and said:

"You go straight to the tram stop, my dear! I think your parents are eager to get away!"

I turned and ran along the road.

And there were my parents, and my father was holding Jutta in his arms. She was crying.

I didn't know whether she had understood what all the fuss had been about, when all she had wanted to do was to get out from between all those legs! But hearing her sobs, combined with the relief at seeing my parents there was too much:

I suddenly found myself crying as well. I held on to both of them and said between sobs that I wanted to go home.

"Yes," Mother said, "I think we'll leave the Zoo for some other day."

And Father nodded and put Jutta down.

She and I held on to his hands, and Mother picked up the basket with the food. There was a tram waiting by the stop, and we climbed in, sat down, got the tickets and the tram moved off. We sat in utter silence, only interrupted occasionally by one of those 'After-sobs' from us two girls.

It felt good to get home, to be safe among our own four walls.

The first thing I did was to wash my sticky hands:

"There!" I thought,"washed off his touch and all!"

Then Mother unpacked the food, and we ate it sitting in the cool dining room. Every now and then, Father would smile at her and then stroke both Jutta's and my cheeks in that special loving way of his. And each time I felt choked with emotion, wanting to burst into tears again....

Later, when Mother had cleared away the dishes and Father had lit his pipe, I settled myself down beside him on the old green settee. I curled my legs under and felt secure once again in his presence.

After he had taken a few puffs from his pipe, I thought I might ask him about some of the strange words I'd heard in the course of the last few days....

He never minded answering my questions, and never lost patience with me. So I started:

"What is a viper, Dad? And a snake pit?"

He explained he had been speaking metaphorically, and I thought that maybe now I could find out what the teacher had meant, when she'd said Hitler would lead us out of the pit!

He gave me one of his indulgent smiles and said:

"Your teacher is what one calls a Fanatic. She thinks Hitler can work miracles."

"Was *she* speaking meta - meta..." I got stuck, it was too big a word!

"Yes, she was speaking ME-TA-PHO-RI-CALLY: She meant the country is in a bad way, like in a deep pit, and that Hitler will get us out of it."

I said:

"Mother doesn't think he's a good man. She calls him an 'Atheist'...what is an Atheist?"

Father explained. He really was a very patient man! And I still kept on, because I just had to know!

"Do you think Hitler just pretends to be friendly? He *did* smile at me when I gave him the roses."

"No, I think Hitler himself is a good man. But he seems to be surrounded by some very strange and nasty people, and that is a bad thing."

"I see."

"Anything else?"

He smiled, patting my cheek.

"Ye-es: What did Mother mean by 'Rough Justice'?"

He took a long puff from his pipe...probably pondering about an answer...then he cleared his throat... and I wondered if he was remembering that SS man....

"It means that someone has been punished UN-justly, or treated harshly or cruelly. But you mustn't worry about it now! Why don't you run along to your camp and see who's won the battle?"

I slipped off the settee and went out to join the gang.

Disenchantment

They were all sitting around the edge of one of the dug-outs. Bernie's team had won... and now Indians and Settlers were having a rest, discussing the fight like old veterans do.

"How did you get on?" Ellie whispered, as I sat down next to her. I said I'd tell her some other time. I didn't feel like talking about it, and was glad when Bernie produced his latest boys' comic. He read us the story of an exciting new adventure, which he said we would use as a guideline for our next game....

So for the time being I forgot about snake-pits and SS men, and on the Sunday I kept my promise to God and went to Sunday School.

After that, my time belonged to the gang....

It was about two weeks later, on a warm summer afternoon.

We were all sitting around by the camp, idly picking blades of grass. We'd had just finished a hectic game of Cops and Robbers and were savouring a kind of tired afterglow.

Suddenly I noticed a strange girl sauntering along the path near the camp, and I saw Bernie's gaze wander across to her.... She stopped a short distance away from where we were sitting and looked at each of us in turn. There was a sort of snooty expression on her face, until her eyes met Bernie's.

He stared at her for a few seconds. Then he called out:

"Are you the girl who's moved in next door?"

She nodded, and he said:

"You can join our Gang if you like. We always meet here."

Well!

Without asking any of us, he was inviting her to join! What was the matter with him?

Then I studied HER: She was taller then Ellie or I. She had blond, short cropped hair, and her dress was sticking out on her chest in two places where Ellie and I were still absolutely flat!

And after giving Bernie a long cool stare, she said:

"I don't play with babies! Where I used to live, we only played kissing games and things like that!"

"Please yourself!" Bernie replied, apparently unconcerned.

But as she flounced off, I could tell from the way his eyes followed her, that he was impressed!

Soon after she'd gone, he said he'd have to go in for his meal now... he'd let us know when he'd worked out the plan for our next game....

But we never planned any more games, and Ellie and I weren't called upon to be chief squaws or anything else any more.

After another week or so, Bernie somehow managed to persuade the new girl to join us. Her name was Silke, she was the same age as Bernie, *and* she belonged to the 'Young Maidens'!

We had all argued hotly about letting her become one of us. And during one of our angry debates, I had sadly remembered the day, when he'd told me that we would have many more battles before the end of the holidays!

But we hadn't envisaged the kind of battles we were fighting now.... I knew I couldn't compete with that girl!

When Bernie had shown her around our camp, the sites of our innocent togetherness, of battles fought and won, she had only said scornfully:

"There you are: Kids' stuff, like I said!"

And after she'd been with us for only a week, during which we hadn't had a single good game, Bernie informed me that unless I let him kiss me "same as Silke does", I wasn't going to be his best friend any longer....

So the battle was lost.

Soon Silke was queen, lording it over all the other children, except Jo and Bernie.

Then the holidays came to an end, and we all went back to school. In our classroom Hitler's picture was gazing at us as before, and our teacher continued to sing his praises, day in day out....

Bernie joined the Hitler Youth, and then the gang broke up.

Not all at once...it sort of crumbled like the unused dried-up clay-pellets, which were no longer needed for ammunition....

I kept away after some of the others, egged on by Bernie and Silke, had began to mock my ignorance about the facts of life.

Then Ellie stayed away as well, and soon the other girls followed suit. Some of the boys still used the dug-outs, but no longer for playing Cowboys and Indians. They were trying out other kinds of games, like the ones Silke was fond of....

I hardly ever saw any of them.

But very soon, Bernie had no more time for his former pals, not even for Jo. When he was not going to meetings with the Hitler Youths, he often went on long bike rides with Silke. And every time they pedalled passed me, I felt stabs of jealousy!

The last time I saw him was a few days before my family moved to another district, where we would be closer to Father's office.

It was on a Saturday.

My parents had decided to treat us two girls to the promised visit to the Zoo at last, and we were waiting by the tram stop, when Jutta pulled my sleeve and said:

"Look, there's Bernie!"

He was marching with a company of Hitler Youths. They were looking straight ahead, singing a song about Germany conquering its enemies, vanquishing all who stood in its way....

I gazed after him and his troupe, still a little sad at the thought of lost companionship....

But then Mother broke the spell, when she said:

"There you are: Bernie's just like your teacher! The two of them are making sure Hitler'll get Germany out of the pit!"

Shadows

I'VE often wondered at what time the fear began to creep in. Not the all-consuming fear that grips you by the throat and threatens to stop your heart from beating....No, to begin with, it was more like a small cloud which passes across the sun.

It soon disappears,and you forget all about it, until another one comes along. Maybe that one is a little larger, a little darker; and as they come and go, their floating shadows begin to convey a sense of foreboding as of an approaching thunderstorm.

But as yet, you don't know when and where the lightning will strike.

Looking back, it must have been during the autumn of 1936, when it began to dawn on me that things weren't as they should be; because the summer holidays of that year still appear as a happy, golden season in my memory. I was twelve at the time, and I still clung to the belief, that *really* bad things didn't happen to one's own self, or one's nearest and dearest, no matter what went on in the outside world.

I had spent part of the holidays with my friend Katie and her cousin Hilde. Katie lived on the outskirts of town.

1936 was the year the Olympic Games were being staged in Berlin; and we tried to copy our favourite athletes on her lawn.

Katie was good at most sports. She was of slender build and she moved with a natural grace, whereas I could best have been described as being big-boned and angular....

The only thing I could do really well was javelin-throwing!

I used to love watching the slender shaft quiver as it stood poised in the soft turf!

But it was the one and only thing I excelled in as far as sports were concerned. Even at school none of the other girls in my class could beat me at that!

Our pretend Olympics were a long way from the P.E.lessons at school, though! There, the non-starters like myself used to be the object of ridicule, even from the teacher....

Sports had become a major subject in the curriculum since Hitler had come to power. Girls were supposed to be turned into strong, strapping females, designed to become the mothers of his future Germany, peopled only by Aryans....

However, Katie, Hilde and I didn't give school a thought during those carefree, happy days.

Nor did we have an inkling that the fabulous show, which the Nazis had staged in the Capital, had been part of a gigantic propaganda effort!

Designed to make all the world believe that things were going well in Germany.

But the games and the holidays came to an end. The athletes and the foreign visitors returned to their own countries, and I, too, went home to our flat in the city.

When I got back, I found an invitation to a party at our Doctor's house. Our Doctor was a Jew.

My sister and I used to play with his two boys, and they were arranging a birthday feast for the following Saturday.

This was something to look forward to!

They had a garden with the most ingenious climbing frames, swings and other outdoor toys. We were sure to have a good time; and even if it rained, there would be plenty to amuse ourselves with in their big play room.

Among other treasures there was an old three storey dolls' house as tall as myself! And then there was the most life-like rocking-horse I'd ever seen.It was as big as a Shetland pony....

Well, it didn't rain, and the party was a great success, but it ended on a sad note.

All Because Of Him

My mother came to collect us, and we said our thank-yous, but before we got to the door, I heard the Doctor say to her:

"I'm glad they all enjoyed themselves, because this may have been the last time."

She was taken aback and asked:

"Why? What's wrong?"

"I'm afraid the future is looking grim for us Jews. Jewish Doctors will soon be allowed only private patients."

"Oh," my mother protested," how will you live? People in this area haven't got that kind of money!"

My sister and I were waiting by the door. I was wondering why both the adults were looking so worried... what WERE they talking about? And what were 'Private Patients', anyway?

I heard Mother say:

"I'm sure we'd all pay as much as we can afford!"

"We'll have to see what can be done" he said.

He smiled sadly as they shook hands.

Then we went home.

Not long after that, I found that the Nazi government's new rulings were about to interfere with my own way of life as well; and I resented it deeply.

I was by now almost thirteen years old and, so far, had successfully resisted the pressure to join the 'Young Maidens', (the female part of the Hitler Youth for the ten to fourteen year olds). Now there was an order making it compulsory from December 1936 onwards! This was accompanied by a threat:

Girls who still refused, would be excluded from the Grammar Schools! It was a shock for many of us.

A lot of my classmates had been marching through the streets for a long time, shouting aggressive slogans and songs. Others were, like myself, still 'unattached'.

What could I do? I didn't want to be expelled, even though I hated Algebra and Chemistry! It was German and English Literature as well as the Art lessons, which I didn't want to miss for worlds....

Then there was the question of our careers: How could we go on to any form of higher education, if we had to leave now?

So I joined.

The others did the same, until there was only one girl left in my form.

Shadows

The rumour was, that she was Jewish and would therefore be barred.

I found the 'Young Maidens' very boring. Most of the time we were assembled in some draughty hall, learning songs and slogans... listening to interminable stories , extolling the virtues of the Fuehrer...and as often as not, rain or shine, we would be marched through the city, bawling wild battle hymns at the top of our voices, singing about flags and blood and revenge....

"What a sight!" I used to think, as we tried to keep in step behind our youth leader. She was a bossy girl of outsize proportions, with an outsize voice.

As often as not, I would ask my mother to write a note, giving some sort of excuse for non-attendance, such as too much homework or a sore throat. But that only worked for a short time. After that the slackers received letters threatening them with expulsion.

That would get them back to square one:

No membership - no Grammar School! So there was no way out. I kept plodding on, staying away as often as I dared.

But all this was no hardship compared to what was happening to some of the people around us.

First of all, the Jewish girl in my class suddenly disappeared. Someone said that the family had gone abroad.

Many wealthy Jews left the country at the time. It was rumoured that they had to pay large sums for their exit visas.

No doubt, the monies boosted the party funds considerably for the next few years!

By and by, many people became aware that the affairs of state were moving in the wrong direction, even though there was less unemployment, and everybody was supposed to take a pride in their work. But beneath the surface there was anxiety in many minds:

What about all those rousing rallies, where Hitler and his chosen were making speeches about the greatness of the Nation, and the need for more space for the Aryan race! There were now more and more threats against the Jews, and there were many harsh new laws!

Slowly but surely, they were enmeshing the ordinary members of the community. Once it had started the process seemed unstoppable because the public weren't allowed to speak out, except in praise of the Party.

Since February 1934 the Party had acquired the power to ban newspapers and thus controlled the press.

But a great many of these new powers and rules were like an invisible net to the citizens: Flies don't see the spider's web, they only realize they're stuck, when it's too late!

I remember the moment when my father first saw the way we were heading. In political matters he had been as ignorant and as trusting as a new-born calf until quite a long time after Hitler had come to power. But then one evening he was sitting in the old green armchair, reading the papers, while my mother was mending one of his jackets, and I was sorting out my books for the next day's lessons. Suddenly he exclaimed:

"Oh, but this is too bad!"

"What is?" Mother asked, looking up from her work, with her needle poised in mid-air.

"Well, it says here, that a man got sacked for criticizing the government. That is interfering with our freedom of speech!"

That kind of news was grist to my mother's mill! She had not changed her mind about 'That Hitler', as she always used to refer to him. So now she immediately put on her 'I-told-you-so-face' and said sharply:

"What did you expect from a man who doesn't believe in God?"

My father knew he couldn't compete, whenever she quoted her highest authority. He answered lamely:

"I used to believe that Hitler was doing his best for all of us, like giving people work and some hope for the future."

"Bah!" She snorted," what future? And as for freedom, there'll soon be none for any of us. You'll see!"

As yet I couldn't see what they were so worried about. Weren't we always told at the meetings that there was a glorious future ahead of us?

On the other hand, if my kind, honest Dad was so perturbed about it, something must be seriously wrong. I wondered:

"Aren't we all free to go where we like and say what we want to say?"

Then I suddenly remembered the Leader at the youth-meetings: Hadn't I been told on several occasions not to question any of the statements about the Fuehrer and his glorious Party? She had said categorically:

"You'd better watch it! To doubt is the same as being a traitor!"

And since then I'd kept my mouth shut....

It was some time after I had overheard my parents' talk.

On my way home from school I came past the street where our Jewish friends lived. I wondered how they were getting on....

"I'll go and see them after I've done my homework."

But when I got home, I found that there must be trouble brewing indeed for our Doctor and his family! Only this time it wasn't something I could just push to the back of my mind!

Apparently, he had sent their young Nursery Nurse to my mother that morning. She had delivered a message.

It had to be a verbal one, because it wouldn't do to put in writing, what he had to let us know....

The young nurse herself was half-Jewish. Jews were not permitted to employ young Aryan women any longer.

As soon as I entered the kitchen, I could tell that my mother was upset: She was ironing, and it was the way she was banging the iron down on my father's shirt front, which betrayed her state of mind!

Unable to guess at the reason for her agitation, I decided it might be best, if I made myself scarce for a while.

I asked:

"May I go to the Doctor's house? I haven't got much homework."

Without looking up from her work, she answered:

"No, you can't."

"Why not? Have the boys got something that's catching?"

"No, nothing like that...."

I saw that she was holding back with the reason but couldn't see why.

"What is it then? Have we done anything wrong?"

"No, neither of you have - but the Doctor sent Nina around today to let us know that it would be best, if you didn't play with them any more."

"But there must be a reason! Please tell me!"

"Oh, there is," she said, still hesitating with the explanation. Guided by her steadfast dislike of Hitler, she probably sensed that there were now pitfalls all around the unwary. At last she put the iron on its stand. Then she said guardedly:.

"You mustn't talk to anybody about this! You can't go because German people aren't allowed to have Jews as friends any more."

"But we've always been friends! We can't stop just like that!"

"We must do as he says," she replied with that note of finality in her voice, which meant she didn't wish to answer any more questions. But then she probably noticed the bewildered look on my face, so she said more gently:

"It would be bad for both our families! And we really must do as he's asked!"

I felt sad. But I knew it would be pointless, to ask her any more questions. I went into the sitting room and started on my homework. It was hard to concentrate with my head full of this latest news....Of course, I had known for a long time that adults weren't omnipotent! But to think that people were so powerless, they couldn't even choose their own friends any longer!

Time went on.

For some months after Nina's visit I don't remember any major upheavals at home or school. Our Doctor still visited us when we needed him; and Mother paid him as much as we could afford.

Life at school had even taken a turn for the better: Since Easter 1937 we'd had a new teacher.

He was to have a great influence on my way of looking at life.

More than that: in later years, he became more like a father figure...and while he was alive, there was always someone I could turn to.

During the Hitler-years, teachers who cared about the ethics of their profession had a tough time. Education was one of the cornerstones of the future Nation. Schools were flooded with memos and guidelines. There was no room for objectors; and, like in any other walk of life by then, there were traps laid to catch the dissenters — but all I knew to begin with was that our new schoolmaster was very unconventional indeed!

Within seconds of appearing in our midst,having greeted us with the obligatory arm-raising of the Heil Hitler Salute, he went to the blackboard and started to write in bold chalky letters:

'Name: Harald Caspers'

'Born: Yes'

'Age: Immaterial'

'Address: Undisclosed'

'Still available: No'.

Well! We were speechless.

What were we to make of THAT?

But some of us discussed it during lunch break, and we decided that it really was a very clever trick: It would stop a good deal of girlish speculations and clear the ground for serious work....

His lessons were never dull. He was a teacher in the best sense of the word; and very soon, most of the girls in my class began to worship him from afar.

It had nothing to do with the usual schoolgirl crushes...we weren't moping about waiting for a smile from our idol — we just seemed to feel we owed it to him to do well!

During the first few months he used to perplex us with some of his questions, and his statements often made us angry...until we began to suspect that his methods were aimed at making us think for ourselves!

Before he came, most of us hadn't realized what marvellous tools our brains were, but now he was making sure we learnt how to use them....

If we answered a question with one of the platitudes we'd been used to, he would give us a quizzical grin, his dark eyes sparkling wickedly behind his glasses, and he would ask:

"Now tell me: Is that what *you* think? Or do you imagine it's what I want to hear? Or because you feel your parents want you to say it?"

He made our heads spin at times. At others he made us laugh at ourselves, when we were slipping back into our old ways of muddled thought and speech.

It was a happy time, not least because we never discussed politics; and yet this fact was perhaps the only flaw in his lessons, if one could call it that: he encouraged us to be open and view things objectively — but because of the political climate, he had no way of warning us that both thought and speech had to be used with discretion. He could not tell us never to be open, nor to criticise where the people in power were concerned!

I don't think any of us girls realized the implications of this. We were happy to do our verbal battles, discussing books, plays, their authors, the way people lived in bygone days and what they thought and believed in....

I only learnt later why he had to be extra careful about voicing his opinions, and why he avoided discussing the affairs of state. But until late in the autumn of 1938 I drifted along, hoping that life might, after all, not turn out too badly.

At home everything continued much as usual. The only problem was my Mother's temper, which had not improved since she'd passed her fortieth birthday. But we were used to her, and we tried to take her in our stride.

Before the terrible events of November 1938, I even found myself hoping that the bad things, which threatened to blot out the brightness, might never come to pass....

Maybe everything would sort itself out one day?

After all, hadn't our friend, the Doctor, so far managed to keep going, even though he was by now only allowed private patients?

We knew that he continued to visit anyone who needed him, whether they could pay or not.

I remembered his latest visit, when he had come to see my father, who'd had another bad bout of malaria.... When Mother had put her usual fee on the table, he had divided the money into equal parts, had pushed one half of it across to her and said:

"That'll be enough."

When she protested, he had smiled at her:

"Look, you aren't rich, and I'm not poor - yet! So let's go halves, shall we?" And Mother had given in gratefully.

I reflected on the many kindnesses he must be doing for dozens of people in our area, day in day out; and not only by day, he still went out on night-calls in an emergency!

I thought:

"And what about the fact that he'd been decorated after the war of 1914-1918 with the 'Iron Cross First-Class' for his services to Germany? Maybe the authorities will make an exception!"

In recent months, my parents had stopped discussing any political issues, when my sister or I were present.

I never read the newspapers.

Until I became too old to have things printed in the weekly children's section, I sometimes used to await the week-end editions eagerly, to see if they had put in any more of my sketches or silhouettes. Once they had even printed one of my stories. But that was a long time ago....

By now I was a member of the 'German Maidens', the 14-18 year olds. It had been an automatic transfer: The 'Maidens' themselves had no say in it. So the Party slogans, the fanatical songs we chanted plus the glowing stories we had to listen to were my only contact with politics. And I felt that was quite enough!

Maybe that was why I had not noticed how dark our horizon had become by the autumn of 1938....

For the Nazi Party, it was only a question of time, of waiting for a suitable excuse to unleash the storm, a storm that was to rage against the Jews and other so-called 'Undesirables', until most of them had perished!

Early in the autumn term of 1938 our teacher had to announce that we would henceforth have to write a political essay on a regular basis. (I believe the titles for them were to be given out by the authorities.)

I daresay most of us thought it was a bore, but no-one said anything. How could one possibly give rein to one's imagination in a political essay?

As it turned out, my first attempt at this kind of exercise was a disastrous failure. And if it hadn't been for the good sense of our teacher, I could have landed my whole family in one of those secret places, which people had only heard of in anxious whispers behind closed doors.

It came about like this:

A few weeks after we'd been told about the pending essays, my sister and I were on our way to school. It was a bright morning in November. My father used to accompany us for part of the way, then he had to turn off to get to his office.

We were nearing a row of shops belonging to several local Jews, when my sister wrinkled her tilted nose, sniffed and said she could smell burning. Father sniffed as well and agreed:

"H-m, it must be quite a way off, because there's no smoke."

We walked on, as yet unaware of the events of the last few hours. But we soon saw. We didn't come across any of the places that had been incinerated during the night, but we witnessed a burning hatred, which would be harder to extinguish than any flames of natural fires.

The storm had broken!

And now we were to see some of the havoc it was wreaking on the victims:

As we came to the first of the shops, we slowed our steps, unable to believe our eyes.

The windows had been smashed. Crystal and glass, delicate porcelain figurines and table-ware lay in thousands of pieces on the pavement, and inside the shop were men in the brown shirts of Hitler's Storm Troopers, (S.A.). They were making sure that nothing remained unbroken! It was a dreadful sight, and it was the same in the other shops.

Many of the owners were known to us. They were all people who had done no more than follow their trade. Some of their families had owned their little emporiums for generations.

My father urged us on, saying under his breath:

All Because Of Him

"Don't stop! Don't say anything! Just keep walking!"

It was difficult. But we crunched our way across the splintered masses of glass, china and crockery, of buckled pots and pans. Even kitchen utensils had been rendered useless by being twisted into grotesque shapes....

Finally, we came to the draper's shop, where the clothes had been torn to shreds and flung through the gaping hole where the window used to be.

The men wreaking havoc in this place were wearing the black uniforms of the S.S.; and they presented the most gruesome spectacle of them all:

They were attacking bales of wool, silk and cotton with fixed bayonets; and since the inside of the shop was unlit, it looked just like a scene from a battlefield, especially as the assailants were accompanying their thrusts with shouts and grunts!

It was revolting...I wanted to be sick... but my father kept on pushing us along over the debris... until we reached the end of the road. There he had to leave us.

"Go quickly!"He said,"and don't talk to anyone about what we've just seen!"

We went off to school and did as he had said: We never said a word about it. I think we were too stunned.

To our surprise, the newspapers printed a glowing report of the terrible events, saying how the entire Nation had risen against the Jewish Adversaries and dealt them a mortal blow!

My parents had long discussions about this, after Julia and I had gone to bed. The walls were only thin, and I could hear them talking until late that night. I couldn't make out most of what they were saying, but the tone of their voices made it plain:

They were worried about this turn of events. At one point I heard Mother mention the name of our Doctor....

During the following week the day of the political essay dawned at last. And lo and behold: The theme about the Jews was on the blackboard!

'How the German people had sacked the Jewish shops and burnt their synagogues.'

Oh, but I wasn't going to have that! I knew who'd done the sacking of the shops! I hadn't seen the burning of the temple, but it seemed pretty obvious to me that the ordinary citizens had been in bed asleep, when that happened. I was jolly well going to write down what I'd witnessed with my own eyes:

Shadows

The shattered windows and the spoilt treasures...the bayonets and the shouting...and the perpetrators in their brown and black uniforms... I put it all down in my furious essay!

And when I'd finished writing, I handed the book to the teacher and thought that would be the end of it.

By sheer good fortune, not one of the other girls in my class showed any interest in discussing the theme afterwards. And this proved to be a blessing in my case. I had no idea what they had written about, maybe they had just repeated the phrases they'd gleaned from the newspapaers....

At the end of the week, when the teacher had marked the work, he made no comment on the other girls' essays, and as he handed out the books, I realized that mine was at the bottom of the pile.

What was wrong?

Even though I hadn't enjoyed writing about the terrifying sights on that walk to school, surely it couldn't be that bad?

To be bottom! Most of the time I was among the top three....

When he picked up my book at last, he still didn't give it to me. Placing it to one side of his desk, he said:

"I want to see you after class. You mustn't make up things like you've done here!"

I shot up from my seat and said hotly:

"I didn't make it up! I saw it! It was——"

But he cut me short:

"Nonsense! You can't have seen it!" And when my mouth opened for further protest, he snapped:

"Sit down, I'll see you later!" And the strange note of warning in his voice made me sink back onto my chair. But I felt angry and humiliated.

How could he? What was the matter with him, calling me a liar, or as good as! Hadn't he always encouraged us to come out with the truth, to speak up for what we believed in? And now he'd made me look a fool and worse in front of all the others!

It wasn't fair!

Then I thought there must be some explanation. I would just have to wait till the end of the lesson. So I sat half hating him for his apparent attack on my integrity, and yet half of me was searching for the reason behind it all....

At last the bell rang, and the other girls left for home.

All Because Of Him

He was still sitting at his desk writing down something in the class book; and while I was waiting for him to finish, I was working out my counter attack: He'd encouraged us to speak out - now I'd show him the results of his methods! I' d make sure he knew that I wasn't that shy mouse any longer, the one he'd coaxed out from a state of permanent trepidation. (At least, I was different in school. At home I was still under Mother's over-strict rule, no use trying to assert myself in *her* presence!)

At last he got up and went to the classroom door. He looked out into the corridor, as if he wanted to make sure that there was no-one about. Then he closed the door tightly.

This was against school rules.

No master was supposed to be alone with any of the girls, unless the door was left open. Our Grammar school had over a thousand girls from ten to eighteen or nineteen years of age. The rule was a safeguard for both teachers and pupils alike, designed to avoid compromising situations.

So what he was going to tell me must be important enough to warrant a breach of regulations. What on earth was it?

Then he came back to his chair and sat down heavily, as if he had a weight on him....But I couldn't bear it any longer, I had to fling my challenge at him:

"I am NOT a liar! I've seen it! I didn't make it all up!"

"Oh my poor child!" He said, and his voice was so full of concern that I suddenly wanted to cry! But I managed not to, and he went on:

"I know you're not a liar, and I do know that you've told the truth! But you CAN'T talk about what you saw, leave alone write it down!"

"But why not, if it's true?" I still didn't understand.

So he explained that if I wanted to stay at this school, and if I wanted to keep my family safe, I must never ever say anything that would contradict the official version of events....

"You see, we no longer have what is called 'Freedom of speech' in our country. And for years now the papers have only been allowed to print what has been approved by the Party. So there's no freedom of the press either!"

I stared at him.

And suddenly I remembered that day my parents had been talking about this thing called free speech...oh, how stupid I'd been!

Now I felt sorry for having hated him, but I still couldn't understand why he'd said those horrid things in front of the class.

"I am NOT a liar ! I've seen it ! I didn't make it all up !"

All Because Of Him

The memory of it rankled even now. I had to ask him; and he explained:

"It was simply that I didn't know how much you'd told the other girls about it. So I pretended that I thought you'd invented it all." His eyes searched my face: "Did you actually tell any of them, either before or after the essay?"

"Oh no,I never said ANYTHING about it to anyone! My father told me not to."

"That's fine then! I'll tear out the essay from your book,and we'll pretend you were absent that day."

With that he pulled out the incriminating pages and tore them into tiny shreds. Stuffing them into his pocket, he promised:

"They'll go into the fire as soon as I get home. And now sit down, while I tell you what happened to me before I came to your school. Then you'll understand how careful we all have to be."

Apparently it had happened a couple of years back, when he'd been teaching at a boys' school in the South of Germany.

"Boys can be less trouble than girls, you know!" He said."With a few exceptions!"

I saw he had recovered his wicked grin by now. Oh, it really did feel good to be friends again! He went on:

"At that college, I had a brilliant Jewish boy in my class. He was good at his work as well as being a decent chap. One day he wrote a really excellent composition, and I read it out to the class like I do here.

The trouble was that there was a lazy, loutish chap in the same class, whose father had a prominent position in the Party. This boy's work was usually near the bottom of the pile. He wasn't stupid, but he never made a real effort. So after I'd read out the   Jewish boy's work, the other one went home and complained. Then his father came to see the Headmaster and demanded that I reverse the boys' positions.

I refused and told him it would be unethical. But then the Head was put under pressure from the man's influential friends: He had to dismiss me!

As a special concession I was given the choice between going to another part of the country, to a school not of my own choosing, or plain sacking and no job....And that's how I came to be among you girls!"

After that, even though I could only vaguely imagine the danger I'd been in, I followed his advice. I even gave up keeping diaries, so I'm not quite certain as to the date of the tragic event I must talk about....

Shadows

It was some time after the attack on the shops.

I came home from school one day and was surprised when my sister opened the door to me without saying a word. She pointed to the sitting room. Then she put her finger to her lips with a sort of warning look, and her face was unusually serious.

The door to the room stood open, and the first thing I saw was Nina, the little nurse. She was slumped forward onto the table, and I noticed that her shoulders were heaving: She was sobbing!

I looked at my mother, who was sitting opposite her. She said:

"You must promise not to tell anyone what we are talking about!"

I nodded, unable to guess what had happened, but it was clear that it must be something terrible, because Mother's face had that kind of look on it. And when she told me, I knew that now the lightning had struck close to home!

Mother said:

"Nina has come to tell us that our Doctor is dead."

NO,no,no! That couldn't be true!

God couldn't allow bad things to happen to people like him! How could he be dead? He hadn't been ill! I could still see him sitting there, at the same place where Nina was now!

Friends couldn't die just like that! And he had been like a member of the family. I had loved him like I loved my Uncle Frederic: They both had that same lovely eye-crinkling smile!

At last I managed to ask:

"But what happened to him?"

Nina now lifted her face to me. Her eyes were red and swollen, and in her hands she had a soaking wet handkerchief. She kept twisting the ends of it. I noticed my practical little sister leave the room, and when she came back, she quietly put a dry hanky into the young woman's hand.

Nina smiled at her through her tears; and then she explained:

It seemed the Doctor had been hoping that Dr.Goebbels, who was the Minister for Culture and Propaganda, might be able to make some concessions. He had thought that perhaps he would be allowed at least a small number of Insurance-Patients....

An interview took place in Berlin. But apparently Goebbels had turned him down flat!

Nina went on:

"I think he 'phoned his wife and told her about it.... But he never said that he wouldn't come back!" And she burst into tears again.

"But how did it happen?" I felt that if I knew it, I might be able to believe that we wouldn't ever see him again.

Nina sobbed:

"He left the train somewhere between Berlin and Hanover. He shot himself with his old service revolver!"

That had been the same revolver he had used to fight for our country in the war of 1914-1918....

Know Thy Neighbour

1941-1944. Up to the time the war started and for some time after, most people passed on political jokes to their friends and workmates, or told them at family gatherings. But as the years went by, you had to be ever more careful and be sure of your audience if you wished to make fun of any prominent figure.

You would check carefully that no-one could overhear as you told a story about Goering, who was so fond of his many medals! (Some were probably quite honestly won in World War 1, but many more were said to have been acquired merely to fill the vast expanse of his chest.)

So one day he visited the steel works of Krupp, and he went missing. After a long search, he was finally discovered dangling from a huge crane: He had been hoisted up by his metal-encrusted front with the crane's giant magnet!

There were many stories about the 'Culture and Propaganda Minister' Dr.Joseph Goebbels, who was a terrible womaniser. People used to say that any aspiring actress had to join him in bed first before she could climb to stardom....But some of the stories about Goebbels aren't printable.

As time went by and the war situation became more and more hopeless, there were more and more jokes being passed around. They seemed to spring up overnight like mushrooms, and no-one knew who had first told them. They tended to become more acid, and they were now told behind closed doors, rather than on the way to work or in a canteen....

Many of the best jokes I remember were brought home by my husband Karl. He was suffering from a heart problem and therefore was not sent to the front until the last few weeks of the fighting.

One evening he came home from the Barracks and said:

"Now they'll all see that the Idol has got feet of clay: they've made it a treasonable offence to pass on political jokes!"

All Because Of Him

"What nonsense," I laughed," they can't stop us telling them to our friends!"

"Ah, but we've got to be much more careful who is listening!"

I regarded him with a reproachful smile and said:

"In that case you want to watch what you say to the woman in the bottom flat!"

"Why?"

"Remember the last air-raid, when we were all in the cellar? She started ranting about the 'devils up there in their planes, trying to murder us all'... and YOU said:'But my dear lady, they are just doing their job! The same as our boys have to do over THEIR cities!' You shouldn't have said that!"

He agreed, saying perhaps he'd overstepped the mark, but he added:

"I don't think she'd tell! She was so helpful last year when your sister died, remember?"

Of course I remembered, but had HE forgotten that the lady's eldest daughter was engaged to a man in the SS?

"AND she's friendly with that funny Party Activist couple down the road!" I added, but he no idea who I was talking about, so I told him:

"They are the ones who say 'Heil Hitler' to each other last thing at night!"

We both laughed, and he promised to be more careful in future...and as it happened, the woman must have forgotten, because no-one came knocking on our door to take us away.

There were now more and more rumours about places where people who stepped out of line were taken to. Of course, people did not talk about them openly, and they didn't know the truth about them; but the fear they inspired was very real to many of us.

There were stories about the Jews, too. My parents and I often wondered if it was true that they were being re-settled in the New Territories, such as Poland?

But there was no-one we could ask.

I remember the first time I heard a mention of that doom-laden name of Dachau; but again, only whispered behind closed doors, as a place where people disappeared to!

It was during the early part of the war... and yet Dachau was the first Concentration Camp Himmler had established in 1933, soon after Hitler had come to power!

Know Thy Neighbour

Had all those Jews who had lived in the blocks of flats opposite been taken there?

I had heard the rumble of lorries during the night, and I had wondered vaguely what was happening.

But next morning, when we opened our curtains, there was not a soul to be seen on that side of the road. Only the empty windows were sort of staring at us....

They had all been taken away!

And yet, even about the saddest things, people sometimes make jokes. Perhaps human nature has to relieve stress by doing so.

I was at a cousin's wedding party, in 1941, when I heard the name of Dachau for the second time: The Best Man had asked, if we would like to hear a new version of the 'Ten little Nigger-boys'?

We all wanted to, and so he recited the saddest little song I'd ever heard.

It was a grim parody. It depicted the so-called crimes of the people who had vanished into the Camps. And instead of the little Nigger boys, it was called the 'Ten little 'Meckerlein', (Grumble-Guts), because to 'mecker' or to complain was considered a crime! Roughly translated, It went like this:

'Ten little Grumble-Guts were sitting drinking wine,
One of them mimicked Goebbels's limp:
Then there were only nine!'

It went on saying how the nine then were thinking seriously about something, (Hitler hated what he called the 'Intellectuals'), and one of them couldn't hide the fact that he'd been thinking, so then there were eight. They made the mistake to write down their thoughts, and one of them didn't burn what he'd written....

Reduced to seven, one of them complained about the food and disappeared. Six of them met a member of the Hitler Youth and one of them called him a 'Lousy Brat', and then there were five....

And so on... with one of them playing a song by Mendelssohn, (who was a Jew), and another telling a joke about the drunkard 'Gauleiter'[1] Robert Ley. Finally the last little Grumble-Guts showed this song to someone...and:

'They took him into Dachau-Camp,
Then there were ten again!'

But no-one thought it was funny. Clever, yes, but far from being funny!

---

[1] A leader of a 'Region', Germany was divided into 35 'Gaue'.

All Because Of Him

And even then, none of us realized that the last poor Grumble-Guts wouldn't have met up with the others again! Because as time passed , the earlier Inmates had to make room for the ones who came later. So for convenience's sake they were killed....

Later, once the German troops had advanced deeply into Russia, there were many anecdotes which showed that people were questioning the sanity of this relentless march further and further into what was then the Soviet Union.

Here is just one of them, probably dating from1942/3:

A little peasant enters a famous book shop and asks to be shown the 'big sort of ball that shows the whole world'....

"Oh, you mean a globe?" The assistant asks.

"Well, one of them round things, what you can turn!"

So he is being shown a large globe, and he says:

"Where's Germany?"

And the assistant points it out to him. Then the little man wants to know which is France, and where is Britain, and he has them pointed out as well, and he nods his head, taking it all in. At last he asks:

"And where is Russia?"

And the assistant's hand moves across the vast country from the borders of Poland to the far reaches of Mongolia, half turning the globe as he does so.

The peasant stares speechlessly for a moment, and then he asks:

"DOES HITLER KNOW THAT?"....

Hitler knew alright!

And by that time millions of people knew that we were trapped, set on a hopeless course. And that there was no way of escape.

There were brave individuals who tried at least to point out the folly of this monstrous war, however risky their remarks were for them. Our History Lecturer was one such, and to this day I don't know how she survived!

I could only think it was due to the fact that she was rather an eccentric spinster, and thus probably regarded as a bit barmy by some of her collegues. So they let her carry on as she did. But she was far from being barmy!

She considered it her duty to warn us, to tell us not to become euphoric, even though our Armies were advancing at an unbelievable rate.... So she would shake us by saying things like:

"Our soldiers are very brave; and we are winning many battles, but we mustn't forget the old saying: 'Many hounds are the hare's death'!'"

At the time I was training to become a Kindergarten Teacher, and there were only ten in my class. I thought most of them could be trusted not to give her away, but could one ever be sure? Luckily, there was only one girl who might have passed on what she'd heard! And she was absent that day.

So our Tutor got away with it!

Over the years people have asked me on many occasions, how the Nazis could literally get away with murder! Why didn't the Germans do something to rid themselves of this diabolical Government?

I believe people who live in a country, where there has always been a free press and therefore also the freedom of speech, cannot imagine what it was like to be deprived of both.

Hitler took away the freedom of the press as early as 1934. And so the deadly net was in position long before the masses became aware of it and felt the pull of the strings! And by then it was too late....

If anyone remembers at all about any revolts, they remember the assassination attempt on Hitler in July 1944.

In my own family, neither parent had a strong interest in Politics, and we certainly weren't told the truth about what went on behind the scenes.... It dawned on me only many years later, when I researched the subject, that there had been numerous attempts to get rid of Hitler and his government even in the early years! Long before the famous bomb blast in his bunker in 1944.

Yet every attempt had failed for one reason or another, and all the people connected with any kind of resistance were executed sooner or later. But these events did not appear in the Press, or, if they could not be hushed up, they were reported in a way which suited the Party....

And during the war Hitler's spy system grew out of all proportions:

In recent years, when I heard about the people in modern China having 'Street-Aunties', who have to be on the look-out for women becoming pregnant after their 'one baby per couple', I remembered the Nazi-Activists who were spying on us in Germany.

They visited the families living in their street, using the distribution of leaflets and such as a pretext to snoop.

Apart from the married couple who said 'Heil Hitler' instead of goodnight-kisses, we had a most unpleasant member of the male species in our street. His eyes were deeply hooded, like hiding things behind their drooping lids. His breath was foul,and his thin pointed nose seemed to draw his head forward in a permanent endeavour to pry into hidden corners. We used to speak of him as 'The Vulture'; I shall say more about him later....

Once we knew who was who, we would limit our chat with that type of neighbour to just a few words, apart from the irksome 'Heil Hitler' Salute. But even then, we had to beware of hidden traps.

I remember one clear night, in a lull between two air-raids, just after the first wave of bombers had finished dropping their load: My father and I had gone outside to check what was happening, when we met one of the activists, not the Vulture, but the'Heil Hitler' one.

This one was a very keen Nazi, but he seemed a decent type of person, and I felt sure he was not an informer. Even so, I didn't like it, when the two men began to discuss the war situation!

A dangerous subject! All but the blindest fanatics could see disaster coming at us like a merciless steamroller! But it would be foolish to voice any doubts!

So I listened with my hand on Father's sleeve, ready to give a sharp pull to stop him from saying too much!

During the past few years he had changed completely. He had been a trustingly ignorant optimist, unable to believe that Hitler was aware of, or to blame for the crimes committed by his henchmen. Gradually he began to see the truth, and by now he was a sadly disillusioned sceptic.

He always maintained that we should be told the facts of what went on around us.

"Truth shouldn't be hidden!" He would say stubbornly.

Oh, he made us tremble at times!

So, too, during that brief interlude, before the next wave of bombers could be heard droning towards us. The Activist mentioned how well the Waffen-SS had been doing on recent battles....

Father cleared his throat. I knew the sign: He felt strongly about the subject... and in spite of giving him a sharp pull at his sleeve, there was now no stopping him! He said:

"Yes, it's easy for the SS! The ordinary soldiers do the tough jobs, fighting their way uphill, dying as they lob the final handgrenades into the bunkers.... Then the Waffen-SS take over and get mentioned in the News as the brave captors of another stronghold!"

The Activist gave him a sort of unbelieving look and said:

Know Thy Neighbour

"But you can't mean that! ALL our Generals are very capable! No matter whether they are Waffen-SS or ordinary Army!"

My father couldn't resist the bait. He said with great deliberation:

"Then can YOU tell me why we hear of the death of some of these high ranking officers in such mysterious circumstances? One of them an experienced pilot! SUPPOSED to have died in a plane crash!"

It must have been Father's lucky day, because the man said very quietly, though with a note of stern warning in his voice:

"Look, we are neighbours; and we are both Veterans from the 1914-1918 War, so I shall pretend that this conversation never took place! But be careful what you are saying, and to whom you are talking in future!"

Just at that moment we heard steps behind us.

It was the spy, the one we called 'the Vulture', and for one breathless moment I thought he'd heard the last remark! But his salute was quite casual, and in any case he had no chance to engage any of us in conversation, because the bombers were coming again.

We went back to our different cellars beneath the flats, where my father gave me a guilty smile. He knew he'd been too daring, but like I said: he'd been lucky this time.

I don't remember when we began to listen to the BBC regularly. I know it was long before 1944. And listening to the BBC became just one more of the many things which were classed as treason.

But I knew many people who did it.

First of all, we had to find the truth about the state of the war. And we thought that the BBC gave us a truer account than our lot. The German News used to talk of a 'successful re-grouping', meaning: Another retreat! So we would listen to the other side and get a rough idea what was REALLY happening.

Just as important as the News were the air raid warnings from the BBC. Most of the time they were given long before our own sirens sounded the alarm. Very often they would state the destination of that particular night's raid: So unless they mentioned Hanover, we knew that we needn't break our necks racing down to the cellar.

BUT, and this was the snag about listening to the voice from abroad:

You had to make absolutely certain that you returned the dial on your radio to the 'Nord-West-Deutscher-Rundfunk'!

It was so easy to forget, especially when the British Announcer had mentioned Hanover as being the night's target, when we would scramble into our clothes and rush down the three flights of stairs. And after a raid, we were sometimes too exhausted too remember that the dial was not in the 'proper place'!

And wherever you lived, be it in town or country, you had to be careful: careful about what you said, and to whom you said it; who you were listening to, and how you answered questions set to trap you.

Half-way through the war, I was staying at my aunt's house, confined to bed with a threatened miscarriage. The Nurse who came daily to give me an injection was a 'Brown Nurse'. It meant she was wearing a brown uniform and was closely connected with the Party.

I dreaded her visits, because, even while she was sticking the needle in my backside, she carried on with her indoctrination attempts!

It was probably because my uncle, who was the Parish Priest of the little village, was known to be anti-Hitler. So the 'Brown' one may have felt that I needed to be kept on the right lines.

But, lying on my face, waiting for the injection, with my nose pressed into the pillow, I had a good excuse for not responding to her tricky Party-talk: I'd sort of grunt a muffled reply....

But, oh, was I glad every time her brown skirt swished out of my bedroom door! Peace until tomorrow....

Then came the summer of 1944, and after the attempt to kill Hitler had failed, there was more spying and prying....

The plot had been so well organized, and so far reaching; the Party Activists were sent to sniff out the people who might have been connected with it, whether on a high or low level!

Even in the barracks, where Karl was no more than a Sergeant, a small group of Officers and some trusted NCOs had been waiting for the Password.... It was tragic to have come so close and then for it all to go wrong.

I remember that afternoon of July 20.

Karl came home earlier than expected. He was out of breath, and without a word he went straight to the radio and turned it on, with the dial set to the BBC.

I was puzzled, because he seemed to have something very pressing on his mind, and he looked different from my normally calm, reserved husband.

Then the voice of the BBC came through, but he'd turned the volume so low, I couldn't get what the announcer was saying....

But Karl could! And he cursed! He actually cursed! I had never heard him curse or use swear words since I'd known him!

"What on earth's the matter?"

He turned to me. His face had gone grey.

"They've failed! They've bungled it!"

"Bungled what? Who's failed?" I was at a loss to understand the violent emotion!

He took a deep breath, trying to talk rationally:

"It was going to be over in a flash: All so well organized, right down to the last barracks! And then they missed him!"

Oh, dear God!

What would happen to the ones involved? No need to ask...it was a foregone conclusion.

"But I don't understand how YOU knew about it!"

He looked at me sadly and said that he could not explain any details, it would be too dangerous for me to know. And I never DID find out how he had been involved....

I wondered how much was known about the small cogs in this giant wheel? It needed just one person's slip of the tongue!

I put my arms around him, and his head came to rest on my shoulder....

When he had calmed down, he said:

"I've got to get back, I only came to tell you not to meet me at the gates, until we see what'll happen."

With that he gave me a hasty kiss and left for the barracks....

It all went very quiet after he had gone.

But no-one came to our door at night....

The German News painted a picture of the Fuehrer's miraculous escape from death; and the Authorities promised to pursue the traitors to the furthest corners of the Reich,(Which by that time wasn't all that far!).

We didn't hear of any arrests among the people we knew; and life seemed to be going on as normal, that is, in our accustomed 'One-day-at-a-time basis....

We kept going to work and listening to the BBC.

We spent a lot of nights in the cellars and hours at a time queuing outside shops for a bit of pork.

About the end of July, while I was alone in the flat, the doorbell rang. I

All Because Of Him

....When I opened the door, there stood the spy—the 'Vulture' !

knew from the way it had been pressed, long and hard, and sort of demanding, that it couldn't be one of our friends waiting out there!

And indeed, when I opened the door, there stood the spy, the Vulture!

My heart did a quick flip, trying to jump into my mouth, but it would never do, to let him see that I was scared. His eyes seemed to probe right into my fast-ticking brain!

He had a bundle of cardboard labels in one hand and was holding on to the door frame with the other.

"Heil Hitler!" He said, "I've come to give you a label to put on your Radio. I expect you know it is treason, to listen to the voice of the enemy?"

I nodded numbly, and he went on:

"I trust you do not listen to the BBC?"

"Oh, no!" I breathed, trying to make my face look guiltless.

He took one of the labels from the bundle, holding it up to let me have a close look at it. His heavy lidded eyes were peering at me as I read its message. It said that listening to the Enemy was treason and stated plainly what the consequences would be....

His wrinkled neck was craning forward, pushing his head closer to me, and, with his thin lips hardly moving, he said:

"This is to be fixed to the dialling knob of your set."

I was about to take the label from him, promising to put it there at once, when he sort of closed his hand over it and pushed past me into the hall.

"No,!" He said. He didn't raise his voice but I felt the menace behind his words. "My orders are to fix it to your radio myself!"

Now my heart didn't jump any longer. It sort of split and sank right to the soles of my feet...it must have done, for they felt as heavy as lead as I followed him into the living room!

My mind tried to race ahead of him, tried to remember who was the last one to have the set on? Had we put it back to our own station?

I had no idea!

All I knew was that within the next few seconds the fate of Father, Mother, Karl and myself was being decided....

I watched him scan the scale at the front of the set, while I said a quick prayer, used for special emergencies. It consisted of only two words: "PLEASE GOD!" I had found it effective many times before. (And since!....)

The 'Vulture' now fixed the notice to the stem behind the knob. He was mumbling to himself....Then he straightened up:

All Because Of Him

"That's done. So you've spoken the truth!"

I told my insides to keep quiet! He mustn't hear the air streaming back into my lungs, as I was getting ready for this huge sigh of relief which wanted to burst forth....

He turned to leave. I followed him out of the room, my knees now feeling a bit jellyish! He was going. Everything was alright! I could sit down in a minute and relax.

But back in the hall, he suddenly turned and fixed me to the spot:

"Oh, one more thing..." he paused.

He had spoken so slowly and deliberately, I wanted to drag the rest out of him, get it over with, whatever it was!

Then he said:

"We know that there were more traitors connected with the plot than we were aware of at first...and we shall root them out, one by one!"

I nodded. My mouth had gone dry, but he hadn't finished yet:

"Do you know of anyone who had anything to do with it?"

I tried to make my eyes look as big and innocent as I could, as I gazed straight at his sinister face:

"Oh, no, we live very quietly, and I don't know anything except what we hear on the News."

(Afterwards, I realized my answer had a double meaning, but he hadn't noticed!)

"Well, if you hear anything, you MUST tell us! Otherwise you are as guilty as the rest!"

And with that he left.

I went back into the lounge and flopped into a chair, trying to collect my thoughts, to work out whether he knew more than he'd led me to believe....

How long before all this would be over?

But our luck held:

No-one came to ask any more questions, and no-one came to our door at night with that fatal harsh knock.

Time went on.

In January 1945 I would be twenty-one. And several months before that, there was an official letter, telling me that as I now was a married woman, I could no longer be a Hitler Maiden...and since I was too old for the Hitler Youth anyway, I could no longer be a member of the over-eighteens group either... (the ones who went by the name of 'Faith and Beauty')....

Know Thy Neighbour

I was to be transferred to either the 'Women's League' or the Party; and I was to let them know my preference without delay!

"Oh, damn!"

I had thought that as I hadn't been attending any of their meetings for a long time, I had managed to slip out of their grasp.

But they had caught up with me! Karl said angrily:

"You don't want to have anything to do with either lot!"

I agreed, but what could I do about it?

"If I can't get out of it, I certainly don't want to join the women's lot," I told him."I might have to go to their meetings with the woman from the ground floor - much too close for comfort!"

From what I had seen of the women, I often felt, they seemed more fanatical than the men.

"Anyway, I don't want to belong to their 'Varicose Veins' Squadron!"

"Their what?"

"Varicose Veins Squadron! It's what we used to call them at college!"

Karl laughed, but then he became serious again and said:

" But you can't join the PARTY! You'd come face to face with the 'Vulture' there and say the wrong thing! You mustn't get caught at this late hour!"

"But if I write and say I don't fancy joining either, they'll come and take me away in any case!"

He nodded, and I managed to make him see that I would try avoid going to any sort of meetings... I should plead late working hours...so I could hardly burn my tongue!

Thus it was settled.

The evening I came home from a sort of ceremony, where someone had pinned a Swastika on my coat, Karl said as soon as he saw it:

"You are not going to walk about wearing that badge!"

"No, but I had to keep it on coming home, several of their lot were going my way."

"I should get rid of it, if I were you."

"Oh, I shall! Never fear, I'm just biding my time."

Suddenly he grabbed me around the waist, laughing:

"Tell you what: The next fine week-end, we'll go for a walk to the Leine-Weir!"

"What for?"

All Because Of Him

I was puzzled. We both loved that walk through the river meadows, where gnarled willow trees were waving their branches close to the dark waters... but I couldn't see the connection with my having become a Party-member, until he said:

"We'll go there and drown the thing! A sort of symbolical end to what it stands for!"

It was my turn to laugh. I thought he was just like a child!

And I told him that as a small girl, when we lived close the Canal, I sometimes used to go there and 'drown' things....

Like the time I had sunk my last lump of pink plasticine, which had been the cause of one of my mother's terrible outbursts of temper: I had got a severe thrashing, only because I had made a small pink appendage from it, in order to change a friend's doll into a 'proper boy'!

Looking back, I seemed to have used the Canal for this drowning ceremony whenever some phase of my life had come to an end....

Now Karl said soberly:

"Let's hope then that this phase of our lives, too, will come to an end soon."

I think we were too close to the approaching collapse of the regime for anyone to bother about the fate of my Swastika badge. And in spite of the darkness at the horizon, the smoke and the rumours, the airraids and the spying neighbours, we could still laugh in the face of the storm.

We thought fate was still smiling at us:

The 'Vulture' didn't come to ask any more questions...perhaps he was deliberately keeping out of sight...we still had each other...part of our home was still habitable...the war would soon be over...and with any luck we might even be alive by then!

So one fine day, we went to the weir and dropped the emblem of doom down the swirling black waters.

Smoke

THE last Sunday in March 1945. A lovely morning with a blue sky. How could it happen on a day like this?

I had woken up early and wondered why I couldn't feel happy at the sight of the sunshine streaming into our bedroom? Why was I being assailed by this overpowering sense of doom?

I reached across to Karl's pillow....

There was no-one there!

And then I remembered: He hadn't been home. He'd had to stay at the barracks for the last night before their departure. And from now on the space by my side would remain empty.

Last night I had promised to see him at the 'Kaserne' first thing in the morning: I would wave and watch them march off...and I would hold back my tears till he and all the others were out of sight.

"Make sure you get there before ten!" He had said, "in case there's another daytime raid."

"I'll be there," I had promised, trying to sound lighthearted, but feeling heavy as lead....

Oh, I must get there in time!

On the spur of the moment, I decided that for once I wouldn't bother taking my hold-all with me. It was such a cumbersome thing, containing some of my treasured note-books, a set of spare clothes and bits of jewellery. For the past two months I'd had to walk to work, because there were too many bomb craters in the streets for trams to operate. And I'd carted that hold-all for two miles every morning and two miles every evening, till it had become a joke with my friends. They used to say that the very day I was to go without taking it, I would lose it in a raid on our area....

But I had laughed and replied that I'd cross that bridge when I came to it!

Well, leaving it behind was to prove a mistake, but as yet I was only concerned with the ordeal of the next few hours, at the end of which Karl and I would have to say good-bye....

After passing through several streets where hollow-eyed ruins stared out from between houses as yet undamaged, I walked through beneath the new wooden railway bridge. It had recently replaced the former metal one after a direct hit.

Then the Goods station.

Once I'd got past that, it was only about half a mile to the big parade ground, where the companies were to assemble.

I dreaded what lay ahead. But I didn't want Karl to remember me looking all sad and gloomy! So I told myself to snap out of this mood of despair and hopelessness....

But what was there to be happy about? The end of the war was looming closer each day. And the thought of the chaos which would follow made everything seem utterly pointless. There didn't seem to be a future for any of us....

Walking as fast as I could, I suddenly remembered the Fortune Teller, who had been reading a neighbour's palm.

Fortune telling was illegal, one of the 'subversive activities', but it went on, nevertheless.... Except that there weren't many Gypsies left to tell them: They had mostly disappeared like the Jews.

Anyway, this particular one had told our neighbour that the whole area through which I had just passed would be reduced to a heap of smoking rubble before the war was over!

Thinking of that prophesy, I now felt a great urge to look back at the scene, which, according to her, would soon disappear....

But then I resisted, telling myself that it was foolish to be worried by that kind of thing!

Perhaps in some remote corner of my mind I still believed that it just COULDN'T happen! Because until it did, no-one could imagine what it would be like! Why shouldn't we get through the last few weeks of the war without losing what was left of our home? It was fragile enough as it stood, with the front wall ripped away, and the front balcony down on the pavement instead of attached to the third floor! For over a year now we'd lived on a sort of slanting level, brushing out the rain as it poured into the whole in the wall....

The back door to our block of flats, too, had been replaced by a bomb crater, damaging the steps which led to the cellar.

It had made it awkward to get down into the shelter in time after the sirens had driven us from our beds. And recently, some of the neighbours had chosen to go to the nearest Public Bunker instead. It was quite a distance away, though,beneath the Wholesale Vegetable Market.

However, my parents and I, (and Karl when he was at home), had continued to shelter in the cellar. But there were times when we were just too tired to make our way down several times during the night, and then we'd just stay in bed, hoping it would be quick, if we'd get a direct hit!

Because of the housing shortage, Karl and I had shared my parents' large flat. We felt we'd managed so far, we'd manage to the bitter end!

By now there were only a few cranks and fanatics who believed that the end would be anything but bitter, that Hitler would come up with some last-minute magical missile....

But Karl had no such illusions:

He believed that the Russians would get as far as the Elbe.

There, he thought, they would be met by either the American or the British Army... whoever got there first!

And only last night he had warned me that whatever happened, I mustn't go across the Elbe, or I would be trapped there!

Thinking about all the 'Ifs' and 'Buts'as I made my way, I had no means of knowing that he was to be proved only partly right!

What he could not have foreseen was the plan the Allies had agreed on: Germany would be carved up in quite a different way from what we expected!

Both the British and American troups DID get to the Elbe on their final push East, but we couldn't have guessed that they were to retreat to the borderline near Helmstedt after only a short spell! Helmstedt was quite a long way into West Germany....

Still, all that was in the future.

For the present, all I knew was, that I had to get through this day, which, in spite of the warm spring sunshine, seemed grey and hopeless....

I reached the barracks, and the sirens sounded just as I was passing through the barrack gates. Karl met me at the main entrance.

"Hurry, I've had the BBC on, they're quite close already."

He grabbed my hand and pulled me down the steps to the cellar.

Surrounded by soldiers all going the same way, we entered one of many large cubicles, each one partitioned off by stout interior walls.

To me they seemed strong enough to withstand any hit!

But we had hardly sat down on the wooden forms lining the walls, when the floor began to rock beneath our feet, the ceiling shook, and the benches we were sitting on went up and down like some fairground machine....

The plaster fell from the ceiling, and then the dust was so thick that we couldn't see across the room. It was like being in a dense fog. The lights had gone out, but there was a greyness coming from somewhere....

Then there was a noise like stones and rocks tumbling, right by the exit of our cubicle. (This was actually caused by the collapse of the cellar-stairs across our exit. But we didn't know it yet.)

Several waves of bombers came and went, casting their loads.

It took about twenty minutes in all. Seen from the air, we weren't far from two main targets: A famous tyre factory and the sprawling network of the Goods Station....

By the time the last planes left, the soldiers in the cubicle next to us were dead.... The ceiling had fallen in on them.

And on our side of the wall, the exit was blocked by a pile of rubble, half-way up to the ceiling. The dust was now so thick, it almost blotted out the shimmer of grey light filtering in above the debris. (It turned out to be daylight, entering by a large hole in the outer wall round the corner from where we sat.)

We were trying to breathe through scarves and handkerchieves, wetted in the water bucket in the corner.

One of the youngsters was crying. He was trying to tie a cloth at the back of his head, but his hands were shaking too much.

Some of them were only just in their teens!

Karl turned to me and said quietly:

"He'll start a panic! Help him and some of the others with tying the things! Try to reassure them."

I already had my own headscarf wound about my face and now tied the

Smoke

boy's handkerchief for him. I put my arm around his thin shoulders, trying to think of something to say, something other than:

"There! There!" My mind seemed to have gone numb.

Then Karl said he would see whether it was safe to leave, and he disappeared in the dust cloud. But he found he couldn't get out of the cubicle, because of the rubble....

He sounded serious but calm when he explained to the youngsters:

"The stairs have collapsed across the opening here. And there's no way out to the right, because that part is down.... I'll open up the break-through on our left!"

He groped his way to the corner where the bucket stood.

Next to it should be the sledge hammer, which was to be used for breaking through the wall:

It was compulsory for shelters beneath houses, flats or other inhabited buildings to have escape routes to the next cellar. Each wall had to be breached; and then a single layer of bricks would block off the opening again. This partition would be plastered only thinly, just enough to stop smoke penetrating, but weak enough for even a child or elderly person to demolish it.

Karl called out to the frightened boys:

"Keep calm! We'll be out of here in no time!"

I heard the clink of metal against metal:

Good! He'd found the hammer next to the bucket.

While he was getting on with the job, I suddenly remembered my parents and the flat...and, like a flash of lightning, the words of the Fortune Teller came back to me!

What had happened at home?

But that worry would have to wait, because it took only seconds for Karl to make an opening big enough for us all to get through.

 He called:

"Come along now, one by one! There's a hole in the outside wall here, only a few feet away!"

The youngster who had been crying nudged me and said:

"You first! Ladies before men!"

I smiled sadly: MEN! These gangly lads were Hitler's last reserve! The round, tear-stained face, with its smears of chalky dust, looked like he'd just come home from school after a scrap with his mates....I felt like giving him a big hug, but it would most likely bring on the tears again!

So we scratched and scrambled our way out, through the wall, up over the debris and into the open....

And then I was overcome by that glorious feeling:

I'm still alive!

I had experienced it before and have felt it many times since:

It can't be described, and it cannot be understood, except by people who, in one form or another, have been through the narrow tunnel of disaster....

I used to wonder whether this was what the Psalmist meant when he talked of the 'Valley of the shadow of death'?

There was less dust out here, and the scene around us was not blurred by the smoke....

It was only too horribly clear!

Around the Barrack Square most buildings seemed to be in ruins. The square itself was riddled with craters, and between the craters the men of the Field-Ambulances were wending their way. They were bearing stretchers with red-flecked bundles on them....

Some soldiers were sitting on the edges of craters. I saw a few of them supporting a comrade who seemed to be unable to breathe properly, and I heard one of them tell the man next to him:

"The silly fool didn't use a hanky, breathed in all the dust!"

Karl and I picked our way through between the many holes, trying to find somewhere to sit.

As I looked at him, I thought how we'd been cheated by fate. What had happened to our last few hours of togetherness before he had to leave? He said:

"I'll go and see what's to happen next. You best sit on the edge of a crater. I won't be long."

We were standing close to some trees by the side of the parade ground, and as he was about to turn from me, there was a huge flash half way across the open space....

I dived behind the nearest tree!

He laughed, like people laugh under stress, when they would really rather cry! Then he put his arm around me and said:

"It's too late to take cover AFTER the flash! But you better get right down into a crater! There may be more late fuses!"

Smoke

So I slid down the side of a big hole in the ground,and when I arrived at the bottom, I just sat.

I sat and waited....

After what had seemed ages, Karl's head appeared above the rim of the crater. He made his way down and sat beside me, breathing heavily. When he got his wind back, he said:

"It seems we're not being moved till late afternoon.... I've got leave until four o'clock!"

"Oh, that gives us a few more hours!"

"Yes, and we'd better see what's happened at home, that quarter is covered in smoke!"

He took my hand and up we went. Getting out of the hole was much more tricky than sliding into it. Most of the time it was one step up and two steps down, but we made it in the end....

Then we walked towards the far end of the square, where the road led back towards the Goods station and to our district....

But after only a few steps into that road we were stopped by a soldier, whose face was blackened with grime:

"No good going any further this way, mate!" He said, "the streets from here on are shut off by fires!"

Karl asked, if he knew how far they'd spread, and the man said:

"As far as the church by the corner of the Wholesale Vegetable Market!" He added that he hadn't been there himself. He had only heard it from people who had made a detour: They'd had to walk all the way around the back of the Main-Line Station in the centre of town!

I had been listening to what they were saying, but had hardly taken in anything after he had mentioned that church:

It was the one at the end of our street!

So the prophesy had come true!

I believe at that moment I was too stunned to feel anything.

We left the soldier and started walking in the direction of the Main Line Station. It really was a long way round, a detour of several miles. There were no fires along this stretch, but a lot of houses were down and the road surface was strewn with rubble.

And all the time while we were picking our way over and around the ruins, I was still clinging to the thought that we might find our home and parents at the end of it.... But then I would tell myself that it was a forlorn hope, and a sort of dull blackness would be all around me...cold and impenetrable....

We came around the back of the station. It seemed to be a shambles, but we never stopped to look.

Then we were crossing the wide approach road in front of it, where some tram lines were stretching upwards in grotesque tangles, and I saw a man who'd had a grocer's shop near us....

I called out to ask if he had any news.

He clambered past the twisted metal and told us that all our street had been one mass of flames, including his shop. He had only escaped being caught in the fires because he'd gone to the big shelter beneath the market.

"What about the people in our street?" I gulped.

"I'm sorry. No-one knows...the heat is too fierce!"

We left the man and carried on towards our end of town. One couldn't really call it walking: We were climbing over fallen masory and blackened beams, stumbling in and out of holes across the shattered pavements.

The state of shock I was in seemed like a veil, making me move forward blindly, following Karl; and every now and then the veil would lift, making me see the scenes around us, as if I was watching something on a distant stage....

I thought the whole city was like a disturbed ant heap: Human ants crawling, climbing, rushing this way and that; meeting one another, moving away again...and above it all an air of agitation, confusion, distress and despair!

Then the thought of my father and mother being in that inferno would suddenly flood my mind, making me want to press on faster.

But it was impossible to hurry. All the streets were filled with spiteful obstacles of one sort or another. We moved in silence most of the time during that agonising walk. There was nothing to be said. We hardly even touched!

The nearness of our parting made touching feel like pain.

When we reached the ancient cemetery near the market, we started to walk through it, taking a short cut.

But it was crowded with people. They were lying down or sitting in clusters on the grass, some with a few bundles of belongings by their sides, others just slumped as if exhausted, staring into space, not seeing anything.

Looking at the pitiful bits and pieces some of them had managed to save, I thought of my hold-all which now was no more!

Smoke

And suddenly, in spite of the depressing sights all around, I had to stifle a laugh....Karl said:

"Can't see anything to laugh at!"

"Nor can I... I just thought of my hold-all: I've carried it for nothing all these months!"

He grinned, and then reminded me that I used to say:

"Things don't matter. It's people that count!"

That was all very well, I told him, but I hadn't even got a hanky to wipe the soot and dust of my face!

"Here, have mine!"

I took it gratefully. (And through all the long months he was away, I treasured that small piece of cloth!)

Winding our way among the crowd, we met people carrying all kinds of containers with some white liquid, some of it slopping over the sides of cans and jugs as they hurried past us.

"Oh, MILK!" I breathed...suddenly realizing how thirsty I was!

And I'd had nothing to eat all day, so I now felt hungry as well!

There was no knowing when or where we would be able to get any food... so Karl said:

"Let's see if we can get some!"

We came to the wall of the graveyard.

There were several farm wagons loaded with milk churns.

A queue had collected, and people were holding up their containers to be filled by men standing on the wagons. It was a strange sight. No money seemed to change hands, and I wondered where the farmers had sprang from. Perhaps it was a remnant of the once so well organized emergency system....

Anyway, there they were, handing out the precious milk...and we hadn't got a cup or can to get a share!

"Never mind," I said, "someone's sure to let us borrow a mug or something for a minute!"

But I was wrong.

We asked several people for the loan of just a small vessel of some sort...and every time it was the same:

They refused, saying that the farmers might be gone by the time they wanted a refill. And when I pleaded with them, telling them that we hadn't had a single drop yet, they shrugged their shoulders and turned away.

All Because Of Him

I looked at Karl:

"I thought people were getting more helpful in troubled times!"

"Not ALL people," he said, and took my arm. "Let's go, it'd be a waste of time waiting here."

As I followed him, away from the selfish mob, I thought that if I had wanted the milk for a child, or someone really badly in need, I would have fought for a cup or a jug!

When I mentioned it, he smiled, mocking me:

"And I thought you were so sweet and gentle!"

"Bah, I've read that there's a dark side to everyone's nature!"

And we left the crowd behind.

Walking past the smouldering remains of the Wholesale market, I saw lots of small black shapes sticking out from the ashes and went closer to investigate.

"I think they are burnt carrots!"

"See if the exposed ends are cool enough to touch," he said, and I pulled out several of the shrivelled things. We blew at them till they were no longer too hot. Walking along, we bit and sucked the few drops of juiciness still contained in their middle. The charred stuff tasted horrible, but the juice was better than nothing!

By now we were only about five minutes walk from our street, and we met yet another person from our neighbourhood. And this time I hardly dared ask whether he knew what had happened at home....

But he must have read the fear in my face, because he gripped my hand and said:

"Your parents may be alright! I saw them walk towards the factory where your father works...just before the sirens went!"

He couldn't tell us, though, what had happened at the factory. But I thought that any kind of relief, even half-relief, was better than nothing!

Again we walked on. I felt as if we had walked for an eternity. The raid of the morning seemed to have happened way back in the past....

And then we reached the top end of our street!

I knew it must be our street, because behind us rose the shape of the church, which sort of pointed towards the entrance with its damaged tower....

Some of the fires had died down, but the heat, as we entered between the blocks of flats, was still intense.

Many buildings had collapsed. Others were only just upright, teetering in that infernal heat, ready to come down any second!

We looked up at each ruin before passing it, and then dashed across in case it decided to crash as we came by....

And then there was our own block of flats, or what was left of it:

Part of the rear wall was still upright. I could see our gas stove sitting on a narrow ledge...and there was a bed ready to slither off a small area of floor attached to an inside wall....

I thought of the many nights when there had been several raids in close succession, when we had been too tired to go to the cellar again and had stayed in bed, clinging close to each other.

Sometimes, then, I had been afraid of just such a thing happening: A bed suspended above the three storeys, waiting to go down with us in it!

We used to say that we wouldn't mind being killed outright!

It was the thought of being stuck on a sort of precipice or being buried alive which terrified us!

Well, we had been spared that experience at least....

But there was nothing here we could do.

The front of the whole block had been blasted away by a 'land-mine', and the groundfloor had collapsed into the cellar.

We could look right down into it, where the tenants' coal stores had been. Now, with their partitions burned away, piles of ovoids formed a glowing mass, throwing out so much heat that we had to move on after a few seconds.

Karl put his arm about my shoulder, trying to comfort me, but for the moment there was still only a feeling of great numbness, blocking out all emotions....

I didn't even feel sad.

He looked at his watch:

"It's time I made my way back to the barracks, because I won't be able to go the direct route!"

"I'm coming with you!"

He shook his head:

"You ought to go to the factory and see if your parents are still there!"

He added that it wouldn't be safe to wander through the burning streets by myself, after I'd seen him off....

But I refused to listen, and we began to retrace our steps back.

A little further up our street, we came upon an unbelievable sight:

All Because Of Him

...Outside the burnt-out shell of their home, sat an old couple...

Smoke

Outside the burnt-out shell of their home sat an old couple.

It might have seemed funny, if it hadn't been so pathetic!

They just sat there on an old settee, holding each other's hands, looking as if they were about to have their photo taken....

Karl said:

"You mustn't sit there! The heat makes the walls collapse! Do go and sit somewhere else!"

But they both smiled, and the old man said:

"We're too tired!"

And the old lady added:

"It doesn't matter if the wall comes down, as long as we are together!"

And they stayed there, smiling....

We hadn't reached the end of the next block, when we heard the crash of the wall collapsing on top of them....

So they were together in the end!

Karl pulled me along towards the top of the street, where we had seen some Prisoners of War earlier on: Italians, Frenchmen, Poles and Jugoslavs. They'd been commandeered to clear rubble and carry away the wounded and the dead.

He wanted them to help dig out the old couple...just in case they were still alive!

With sign language and nods and headshakes, we managed to make them follow us to the pile of bricks and charred beams....

They shook their heads at me sadly and said:

"No sight for lady! Soldier take her away!"

And they started digging while Karl led me towards the church again. But another wall came down some way ahead of us, and we turned into a side street, hoping it wouldn't be blocked as well....

We had hardly entered it, when we came to a huge pile of burning ruins, which I remembered as the place where the drug store used to be.... And from it, through gaps and along beams, flames were licking their way into the open... licking as if they were trying to catch at our clothes, and the blazing heat emanating from the pile felt as if it would melt our very skins!

We were still trying to find a way past, when we realized that besides the crackle and the hiss of the flames there were other sounds rising from the inferno:

They were screams!

Screams that came from beneath the rubble and the fire....

Families with children had lived there:

They were being burnt alive!

Karl wheeled me round and pulled me away:

"Don't listen! We can't help them!"

And again I folloowed him blindly, turning back into our own street....

We were just in time to see some Italians carry away the old couple on stretchers.

They were covered up.

The prisoners nodded to us, a kind of sad salute...and I gritted my teeth at the futility of it all!

Why couldn't mankind manage to get on with living instead of all the killing!

Near the top of our street Poles and Frenchmen had by now made a narrow path through the debris, and we trudged back the same way we had come. When we got to the cemetery, the farm wagons had gone. The place was almost deserted.

On we went.

I can't say how long it took to get to the Barrack Square.

When we arrived, we saw groups of soldiers standing about, waiting for orders, almost ready to leave....

Names were being called; and to some there was an answer, others were followed by silence... and the officers, who were attempting to sort out who was missing and who was not, made marks on their lists accordingly....

A soldier detached himself from one of the groups and came over to us. He said to Karl:

"Someone brought a message for your wife: Her parents are safe. They are waiting for her in the cellar of the factory!"

(Later, when I saw them at last, they couldn't say what had made them decide to go to there. It was the only time they had ever gone to a shelter other than their own cellar....)

If only the relief I felt hadn't been overshadowed by this feeling of doom!

Within the next few minutes I would have to leave Karl, knowing that I might never see him again!

He said hoarsely:

"We'd better say good-bye now. It may be a while before they've got everything in order. And you MUST get to the factory before it gets darK!"

I knew he was right.

But every part of me that was still able to feel ANYTHING cried out against my doing as he asked!

And I was so tired! I wasn't even sure I'd be able to walk as far as the factory! After all, neither of us had sat down since the morning, when we'd briefly rested in the bomb crater!

But the time had come, and the dreaded moment passed... one last kiss, and I left him standing at the edge of the square... we had both agreed not to turn around and wave....

But then I got to the corner, where a gap between some ruined houses marked the entrance to the road I had to take, and I couldn't resist!

I looked back.

He was still standing on the spot where I'd left him... and so we waved once... and then I turned the corner.

The fires were mostly out in this street by now. Only a glowing warmth glimmered above the heaps which had been homes when I passed them earlier on. But as the sun had gone now, it was not unpleasant to feel that warmth....

By this time I was more stumbling than walking.

I was glad that I'd put on my handmade high boots when I'd left home that morning. They supported my tired feet better than shoes would have done; but even so, the way seemed so much further than before!

When I was nearly at the Goods Station, just round the corner from the newly built wooden bridge, I saw that the road was flooded. And before I'd gone much further, it became clear that I would have to face yet another obstacle: The bridge was lying half in the water, and the parts that weren't wet were on fire.

I thought that the water in the dip below the bridge might be deeper than the top of my boots. Even though they were waterproof, from now on they were all I had to wear; and I didn't want to get blistered feet if the inside leather got soaked!

So I decided that I'd climb over the railway embankment....

I retraced my steps to where I had seen a hole in the fencing earlier on, intending to claw my way through it, when I heard some one shout from above. Looking up,I saw a man in railway uniform standing on top of the bank. He said:

All Because Of Him

"Don't come up here, please!"

I thought it was a strange request, especially as he'd said please! But I wasn't going to be put off and called back:

"I've got to get to the other side, and the road's flooded!"

"DO go through the water, it isn't all that deep!" His voice was almost pleading, but I couldn't see why, so I insisted I'd rather go over the top where he was....

"My Dear, " he said, "do as I ask! The place up here is full of torn corpses! There are arms and legs and everything else strewn about... a Red Cross train has been hit!"

Oh God! Was there no end to the horrors of this day?

I thanked him for telling me, then went back and started walk ing through the flood. If I went very slowly, without making much of a ripple, my boots might just be tall enough to keep the water out!

The beams of the bridge were burning fiercely, where they were still attached to the dam. So I climbed over the part that was submerged and managed to get through the murky waters with my feet still dry. And, from old habit, I thought:

"Thank God for small mercies!"

That was the moment, when the build-up of events during the day struck me for the first time!

All the horrors seemed to rush in on me like a tidal wave...and I found myself asking the question mankind has always asked at times of tragedy:

"WHY?"

I wanted to know how God, who was supposed to be a 'Loving Father' could let things happen to innocent people?

Even if you didn't count the tragedies involving adults in all the coun-tries caught up in the war... what about those children?

Burning alive, with their mothers powerless to help them?

Why did HE let it happen?

And then I thought that He might not even be there: After all, he cer-tainly had no resemblance to the one I'd been told about as a child!

I could only feel emptiness, where the image of a loving father should have been....

And as I stumbled along, I suddenly realized that my face was wet....

And then for a long time I couldn't stop the tears.

I carried on, hardly seeing where I put my feet... sometimes falling over pieces of wood and heaps of bricks...and each time it became harder to pick myself up again.

But it couldn't be all that far to the factory now. I knew that somewhere ahead I would have to cross a large open square, and after that it would only be about half a mile or so further. I also knew that I would have to get there soon, I was barely able to lift my feet, and was staggering from one near-fall to the next!

The streets were deserted. Gradually, a kind of apathy was beginning to lull my senses. I thought:

"Next time I fall, I might just stay put! Maybe they'll find me, when they come to clear away the rubble!"

But just before I reached the square, I heard footsteps.

They were coming from some side street... made by many feet... and they were now entering the square just ahead of me:

It was a group of French prisoners on their way back to their camp; and I had this hunch to join the last row of them, just to be close to some living souls!

They didn't seem surprised to see me in their midst. The ones next to me gave a sort of soot-and-grime-stained, tired smile; and I smiled back, trudging a little faster than before to keep up with them.

I was no longer looking ahead or sideways, just sort of a foot in front of my boots.

But somehow it felt safe not to be by myself in all that desolation; and suddenly my mind went back to the French prisoner who had come to repair our bomb blasted windows about two years ago. He and I had had a talk about the pity of it all, and I wondered what had happened to him? According to the rules, he and his fellow prisoners were supposed to be my mortal enemies!

And yet here I was, drifting along with his countrymen, being grateful for their company!

The one who had fixed our windows had told me he came from Marseilles, and that he had a wife and two children.

One of the things I remembered him saying was that wars and injustice bred more wars and injustice, no matter whose side was in the right, or whose side won....

I had protested:

"But what about people... all over the world... you and your family... me and my family...why should we hate each other?"

He had smiled, a sad smile:

"Not People! Politicians and propaganda! They start it!"

I had given him some sandwiches, a piece of cake and some apples to put in his tool box, putting my fingers to my lips, saying:

"Sh! Hide it!"

And again he had smiled, but this time it was more a kind of conspiratorial grin:

"Look!" He said, lifting a piece of cloth which was covering the lower compartment of the box....

And there were more pieces of cake, more sandwiches and more apples!

I must have looked surprised.

So he said:

"You see? People good! Many good! Should shoot politicians!"

And now, traipsing along with his compatriots, I was sure he'd been right!

But oh, I was so weary, I felt like falling asleep on my feet....

We were about half-way across the square.

It was surrounded by burnt-out shells. Behind the blackened facades flames were still flickering across remnants of beams and floorboards. But I hardly saw any of it. I was only vaguely aware   of the sights and sounds around me: All I wanted was to get through these next few minutes, and to find a place to sit down....

Suddenly, there was a shout from the leader of the group!

The prisoners came to a standstill so abruptly that I bumped into the back of the man in front, reeling after the impact; and if it hadn't been for the steadying arm of the one next to me, I would have fallen. But he held onto me until I was firmly on my feet, and when he let go, he smiled.

Then we heard this sort of cracking, rumbling sound ahead of us.

There had been a three storey block of flats across part of the far side of the square, and the leader had realized that it was about to collapse....

The wall facing us was breaking up!

It happened almost in slow motion... it was swaying forward and back...as if determining which way to fall... and then it came down towards us like a load of children's bricks... tumbling and tottering... and finally crashing onto the space ahead of us!

Some of the pieces of masonry stopped rolling only feet away!

Smoke

A sort of hot stone avalanche....

If it hadn't been for these prisoners, I would probably be beneath that avalanche now!

No-one spoke.

Once the wall was down, the man in front called out something in French, and the whole column moved forward again, with me among the last stragglers.

After another few minutes we reached the gates of the factory.

I uttered a few words, remembered from French lessons of a long, long time ago, and the ones nearest to me said:

"Bon nuit!"

And as I walked away from them towards the gates of the factory yard, I heard them call out:

"Bonne chance!"

Yes, I certainly needed that!

It was getting dusk as I reached the cellar.

The large room was cold, illuminated by just one bulb. I recognized some people from the office and the printing floor, who were sitting on bunks and chairs.

And then I saw my parents:

Had they looked as old as that, when I left them this morning?

But my father's face lit up, when he saw me, and Mother slowly raised her tired eyes and came forward to make sure it was really me....

We hugged each other in a sort of threesome, tension now dissolving into tears of relief....

Then Father stroked my cheek, murmuring soothing words, which reminded me of days long ago, when I'd been hurt; and Mother just held on to my arm, sort of making sure she wasn't dreaming....

In my childhood years and as a young adult, I had never been close to my mother:

She was dominiering and quick to anger. Yet I think that beneath the surface she often felt insecure, and then she would try to compensate by undue harshness....

I had always been afraid of her temper!

But now, seeing her sitting there, I thought how utterly lost she looked, in a kind of homeless vacuum.

My heart went out to her, and I found myself wishing I had the power to make life ahead easier for both her and my father!

A little later, I went to the corner of the cellar, where there were several washbasins and I washed my face.

I washed off the grime and the soot; but the smell of burning clung to my clothes for ages.

And the memory of that day clung to me for life....

The day my faith in the God of my childhood was buried under the ashes, when we heard the children screaming in the smoke....

Waiting

APRIL 1945. The village lay quietly in the warm spring sunshine, but none of the inhabitants ventured far beyond their own farmyards. No-one wanted to be caught away from home, when the American tanks were going to roll in. And as the hours went by,the very air seemed to become electrified with the tension which had us all in its grip.

The three of us sat in the farm kitchen. There was Martha, whose husband owned the farm, there was Hilda, her sister in law, who was staying there to help out, and there was I, who had meant my visit to last for only a couple of days. But the two of them had persuaded me to stay: They had admitted that they were terrified of what the next few days would bring.

They had obviously been affected by the many horror stories, which were put about by our own government. So I had thought it over and decided to remain. Now we were waiting like the rest of the villagers. Like many of them, we were praying secretly that the Western Allies would get here soon.

We were not far from Magdeburg, and everyone was afraid that the Red Army might get across the river Elbe, before the British or the American Soldiers reached us....

"What day is it?" Martha asked, and I answered:

"Friday the thirteenth. I've just checked with my diary."

Hilda remarked that it was an unlucky number, and then we sat in silence again, straining our ears, each sound from outside making us jump.

The two young women were both in their mid-twenties, a few years older than myself. They were my husband's cousins, and I had only known them for a short time.

Sitting opposite them,I studied their faces: Martha's was rather plain, a sort of open face, surrounded by frizzy blond hair, which she was apt to fidget with when she got agitated. At the moment, however, she was much calmer than Hilda.

Hilda had married a 'Townee' and had become one herself, to judge by her looks and her clothes. She was usually a happy go-lucky kind of person. She, too, had blond hair, but hers was permed, and even when she had just emerged from the cowshed, she didn't look like a typical farmer's daughter any more.

But today she was not her usual self.

She kept dashing upstairs to the attic window, every time there was a rumble in the distance. There was a white sheet lying by that window, ready to hang out as soon as we were sure of the Americans' imminent arrival....

She sighed:

"I wish we could just hang out that sheet and leave it there!"

But we knew we couldn't, because at the top of the street, there lived the fanatical Burgermaster, who believed even now that Hitler held in reserve some special weapon which would turn the tables!

Only a few days back, he had told a neighbour that he would personally shoot any traitor to the cause! And that very morning we had watched from our front gate, how he had taken delivery of some hand-held anti-tank guns, called 'Panzer Faust', meaning 'Tank Fist'. The things had the look of an outsized hand grenade, fixed to the end of a kind of long hammer hilt.

We heard him say something about distributing them to the farmers just before the tanks reached the perimeter of the village. It was a crazy idea!

We felt it could only be a question of hours now.

The heavy guns,which had thundered some distance to the West last night, had stopped firing long before dawn. So it seemed that there was no more resistance, and I tried to imagine how the victors would enter the villages. I prayed that there would be no more shooting!

My mind went back to the day when Martha had issued her invitation to extend my stay. She had asked:

"Why cant you wait here with us, till it's all over? After all, you've got nothing to lose!"

Dear Martha! Her last remark was perfectly true, even if not very tactful: Considering that I had lost all my possessions in one of the last air raids on Hanover, I was as poor as the proverbial church mouse and as free as a bird!

She and Hilda had taken me all over the farm house soon after I had arrived. People in that part of the German countryside had not experienced much hardship up to that time. So the two young women had proudly displayed their treasures to me. They were only following an old custom among farmers: You showed off your dowry, (that is, if you had any!).

I'd had to smile to myself, as they led me from room to room, opening and shutting drawers after drawers, and so many wardrobes that I lost count.

There was enough bedding to furnish several hospitalwards! And there was linen of the finest quality. One huge cupboard contained bales of woollen cloth, to be made into whatever they might need in the way of suits and costumes... and there were clothes and nightgowns, shoes, stockings and satin underwear, enough to fill a shop!

I thought wickedly of a verse somewhere in the Bible, something about treasures that get eaten by moths and rust! Well, here was a feast for them!

But neither of the two women had wished to hurt my feelings. It was just thoughtlessness. Apart from their pride in things that didn't really matter, they were kindly people.

I thought it was probably because their world was falling apart and their wealth was the only tangible support to cling to....

They had told me that neither of them could understand how calmly I had accepted the loss of all my possessions, and when I said that, after all, it was the same for millions of people all over Europe, Hilda had asked:

"But how will you manage, when the war is over?"

I had shrugged my shoulders and told her quite calmly that I'd not really had time to think about that yet... and both of them had stared in horror!

Then Martha had gasped:

"I would rather die than lose all my dowry!"

Perhaps it was unkind to laugh at that statement — but I just couldn't help it!

"Possessions are only THINGS! They aren't worth dying for!" I'd said, and then, to smooth it over, I told them that I was a long way from wishing to die:

I wanted to go on living, wanted to see what would happen next!

And there was always the hope that Karl, my husband, would come back one day....

"Surely, that's more important than the loss of mere things?"

Both of them had to agree, because, like me, both of them were waiting for a sign of life from their own husbands.

But I felt certain that their wealth would always be like an idol in a shrine to them: The figures of their husbands only just a fraction larger than their Tin-Gods!

However, after we'd finished the grand tour of their house, they DID give me two used sheets, both with pretty patterns on them, so I could make myself two summer frocks!

When Martha handed them to me, she asked temptingly:

"Would you like to sew them while you are staying with us? You can use my machine!"

When I hesitated, Hilda had added:

"Do say you'll stay! We're all in the same boat! I mean with none of our husbands around...I think the three of us should stick together."

I remembered something she had said earlier: She was sure we were all about to be raped or murdered, or both.... And it suddenly occurred to me how lucky I was in spite of all that had happened:

My own upbringing and the foresight of Karl, who loathed the Nazis, had helped me to look at events objectively. At least as far as the soldiers of Britain and America were concerned....But I also remembered how, when we were about to part, he had warned me:

"Whatever you do, don't go across the Elbe, or you'll be stuck there!"

I was to remember those words many times in the years to come.

But for the time being, I was staying with the cousins. It had been gratifying to see the relief on Martha's face, when I had agreed to stay.... And then we'd all had to laugh, when Hilda had winked at me and said:

"You know, she's got an ulterior motive. She thinks you'll be useful, when we need an interpreter!"

"I thought there would be a catch somewhere!"

I was glad to feel welcome, although I didn't think that they would want anyone to help with chatting to the victors! Even if all else went well, fraternization would be a long way off!

Waiting

I'd been here for almost a week now. And every night the skies had become redder and redder with the nearing of battle. Much of our time was spent in a state of lethargic tension: Only things such as milking the cows and seeing to the needs of the livestock were being attended to.

We dared go no further than next door, just to discover, if they had any fresh news other than we'd heard ourselves....Rumours were flying about like Dandelion seeds, fanned by hopes and fears alike.

It was about ten o'clock in the morning, when Martha got up from her chair. She stretched her arms, almost touching the low ceiling, and said:

"I'll make some coffee! Maybe the smell of it will bring Vladim to the door! I was hoping he'd give us a hand with the pigs!"

Vladim was their Polish prisoner, who had helped with the heavy work since Martha's husband had been called up. Apart from the Pole, both the young women had managed on their own.

During the last few days we had seen less and less of the young man. Like most of the other Poles, he had decided to turn up only when he felt like it. This generally meant he did a little work towards mealtimes: Just enough to make us feel he had earned his lunch.

All the prisoners knew that events were hurtling us towards the big change. We were well aware that they had secret meetings. Some of the German guards at their camps seemed to have fled days ago. Who could blame the Poles for becoming restive?

There were only a few farms where they still had to toe the line: Some of the fanatical Nazis still acted as if they owned their prisoners body and soul....

But the Poles knew that their time was at hand.

Hilda now said:

"I don't think he'll show up any more today. He was muttering about those Panzer-Faust things, when he'd finished milking this morning. I think they're going to discuss the Burgermaster!"

"Do you think they'll manage to stop him?" Martha asked.

"I'm sure! He's told me that they're ready for anything!"

I shuddered. The Burgermaster was known to be a brutal task master to his foreign workers. Vladim had said:

"He's a swine. He's got it coming to him!"

I knew the Poles meant it.

It was this kind of atmosphere and the feeling of uncertainty, which made our nerves act like bell wires: The slightest touch would set us jangling!

So the morning wore on, and while we were waiting, the village street suddenly became like an unreal open-air theatre. There were long intervals between the different acts, but each one of them has become etched into my memory forever.

First on the scene were two weary German soldiers on foot. They were covered in sweat and dust. It was difficult to make out their features apart from their eyes: They were huge and bloodshot from lack of sleep, grime and exhaustion.

Hilda had first spotted them from the look-out upstairs, and had come rushing down to tell us. Now we watched from the kitchen door as the two of them came slowly trudging along the cobbled road.

I remember thinking that their feet must be full of blisters.

Martha went to the farm gate, swung it open and called out to them. And as they painfully made their way across the yard, she said:

"Oh, you look dead on your feet!"

She led the way into the cool kitchen, where they sank onto the wooden corner seat. Seeing them close by, I thought:

"They're hardly more than boys!"

They were too weary to talk. They just sat there, gazing at us. Then a kind of puzzled look came over their faces, as if they couldn't quite take in the normality of the place: The everyday objects of a clean farm kitchen, with all its usual implements for cooking and housekeeping, all hanging on the walls or standing on neatly stacked shelves.

Silently, Martha went to the dairy and fetched a large pitcher of fresh milk.

They emptied several tumblers full in complete silence.

They didn't gulp, they drank as if drawing deep breaths, slowly, like a horse takes long draughts. It seemed that new life was flowing into them as the cool liquid ebbed from the glasses....

Then they wiped their lips with the back of their hands and sighed. A deep, contented sigh. One of them said:

"We haven't tasted milk for weeks!"

"We haven't seen cows for weeks either," his companion added, and Martha explained that here, in the heart of the countryside, the effects of the war had only recently begun to bite.... Most farmers had had enough to eat, and to spare.

"Mind you, most of them wouldn't admit it!" She laughed, then she asked them to stop for a meal.

But they refused, and I thought:

"Maybe it's better if they don't hang around here! What if the Burgermaster should appear on one of his phoney visits?"

Since the failed attempt on Hitler's life in 1944, some Party activists had made it their business to check on their neighbours. I still remembered such visits to our flat in Hanover....

No, the Burgermaster mustn't find those soldier-boys in Martha's kitchen!

She probably had similar thoughts, because she changed the subject and asked where they were heading for.

"Anywhere where the Americans are! They can't be very far from here now." Said one of them. And his mate added:

"We've got to give ourselves up. Our company was wiped out during the night."

There was a silence. It seemed filled with the horror of the memory.

I guessed that they didn't wish to re-live those hours by thinking or talking about them. So I said:

"But you must have walked around in circles, arriving here from an Easterly direction! The Americans are still some miles to the West!"

The one who seemed to be a little older than his comrade said wearily:

"It was dark. We lost our bearings after the shooting stopped... we couldn't tell where the Amis were... so we came across fields... and when it got light, we realized we were too far East!"

The other one shifted his aching feet and sighed:

"And we haven't stopped walking since!"

"Why didn't you just wait by the roadside, instead of walking your legs off?" Hilda asked. "The Americans will catch up with you sooner or later!"

"We daren't risk that," said the older one, "there are still a lot of Waffen-SS men lurking about. They'll shoot anyone who isn't with his unit!"

He went on:

"We didn't want to wait too close to the Elbe either, in case the Russians get across before our lot blow up the bridges."

I asked:

"But who'd do that at this stage?"

"The SS. It's part of their policy: To leave behind nothing but chaos....

All Because Of Him

Oh, what a mess!"

There was a long pause.

Then he asked very quietly, as if daunted by the enormity of the request he was about to make:

"Would you be willing to let us have some civilian working clothes?. It might help, if we did come across anyone from the SS."

It was such a simple thing to ask for....

Yet we knew that if we were caught, it would mean instant death!

But Martha and Hilda didn't hesitate.

Maybe they were thinking of their own menfolk caught in the same plight? They disappeared to rummage through their husbands' working clothes, while I stayed with the two men. No-one spoke.

But their talk had opened a terrifying prospect, as far as my own family was concerned: My mother was on the other side of the river Elbe! My father had taken her there after they lost their home. Now she was staying with her sister in a village East of Magdeburg.... Father had returned to his work in Hanover. He was going to live in the cellar below his office.

He had been convinced that the Russians would stop at Berlin! To him it was unthinkable that the Western Allies would let the Red Army get further than the Capital!

Even Karl hadn't been able to make him see sense....

And now I realized that I was as terrified as the cousins were, only for different reasons. I thought:

"How will Father get her back, if the bridges are blown up? And how can I go looking for her, if I can't get across?"

The thought of what might happen over there was unbearable!

Waiting for the Americans was daunting enough! Yet everyone I knew would rather fall into their hands, than be in a place that was being overrun by a victory-crazed Soviet Army! Oh, it was a hopeless prospect!

Then the two women came back with an armful of clothes as well as a pair of shoes for each of the men. They got up and took the clothes almost reverently... and Martha said:

"You can change in the barn. There's a pump there and a towel, so you can have a wash."

"I'd better show them the back-gate," Hilda suggested,"then they can slip into the copse and make their way across fields for a mile or so!"

"And remember to go West!" Martha said with a smile.

Waiting

"One more thing," the older one said," may we have an old sack each?"

When we looked puzzled, he explained that they wanted to hang on to their uniforms.

"As soon as we see the American tanks, we'll change back into them!"

When they left, they looked so relieved and so grateful; but I was afraid for them. They had been thrust into this whirlpool of impossible goals and hopeless confrontations. Would they make it to safety?

After they had gone, we sat quietly for a while. There was still nothing to do for us but wait, and for Hilda to keep darting up to the attic, whenever she fancied she'd heard an unusual noise!

After the two soldiers had departed, Martha had decided to leave the gate wide open.

"There'll be more people needing help,"she had said, "and it looks more sort of welcoming!" Then she'd put her biggest kettle on the old range, ready to make coffee at a moment's notice.

We didn't know yet that the people who would have needed our help most, were beyond human assistance! But that part of the drama came much later in the day.

The next sounds from outside came from the engines of two Red Cross Ambulances. It was about noon when they stopped at the farm gate.

The drivers, one young Corporal and an Orderly, came to the kitchen door, and the Corporal said:

"The men we've got with us can't walk. Could you let us have an old milk churn with water to take with us?"

"Yes, of course!" said Martha, who was always happiest when there was work to be done.

"But none of you'll leave before you've eaten!"

She welcomed the chance to fill the idle hours of waiting.

So Hilda had to fetch one of the churns from the dairy, while I was told to get the home-made butter and a couple of liver sausages from the pantry.... Then, with her sleeves rolled up, the young mistress of the house set about cutting slice after slice off large round country-loaves of bread, and we made piles of sandwiches and took them out to the wounded.

Next she ordered:

"The men can fill the churn at the pump. And you two better take the coffee out to the others! After that, we'll eat ourselves."

When the two drivers came back into the kitchen, we all sat around the clean, scrubbed pinewood table. The steaming hot coffee pot was waiting. It was only 'Ersatz-Caffee', but who cared?

We all tucked in and ate, till there were no sandwiches left.

Between mouthfuls, we talked about the state of the war....

I thought that Hilda was anxious to ask the question which had been uppermost in her mind all along...but she probably didn't know how to start....

At last, when she'd finished eating, she turned to the Corporal, her big blue eyes showing her fear:

"What is going to happen to the women in the occupied villages?"

The Corporal gazed at her thoughtfully:

"Nothing," he said, "unless the women want it to happen."

"But they say we'll all get raped!"

"Who are 'THEY'?" He asked, and then, as she hesitated, he smiled and said with a hint of irony:

"I see you've been got at by Party-propaganda!"

His statement made the three of us quickly glance at the kitchen door! It was open, but there was no-one there to overhear. So he went on talking to us, quietly, like an older brother; although I thought he could be no older than the cousins.

Hilda's anxiety was obvious. Her hands were endlessly twisting and then smoothing the frill of her pinafore.

And it was plain to see that Martha was in what she would normally have called 'a proper state': She was pushing the crumbs which were left on her plate round and round with one finger, stopping every few seconds to push back some wispy bits of hair from her forehead....

The corporal now said:

"Really, you surprise me! Intelligent young women, able to think for themselves! And here you are, quaking in your shoes! The Americans and the British soldiers are no different from our own men! They won't harm women!"

"But they have Negros in their Army!" Hilda protested, and he looked at her long and hard:

"So-o?"

"Well, I mean, they are not civilized, are they?"

Another long look, I wondered if he was weighing up his next words, because, after all, he couldn't be sure that none of our husbands was in the

Waiting

SS, or even the Gestapo....

Then he said:

"You mustn't think of Negroes as monsters. That is just another fabrication of the Propaganda machine! And as for being civilized! There are things done in any war, and on BOTH sides, which cannot be called civilized by ANY standards! It's got nothing to do with race or colour!"

Up to this point I agreed with him: I had read 'Gone With The Wind' just before I was bombed out. I had borrowed it from my old schoolmaster from Grammar school days. He had handed it to me with a warning:

"Don't let anyone know you're reading it! It comes under the heading of subversive literature!"

The book had been a revelation. It had made me wonder, why mankind hadn't learnt from history. And it had also shown me the stupidity of the white races regarding themselves as superior!

I wasn't worried about black soldiers.

I was troubled by stories that the Allies had attacked Red Cross trains.... There had to be an explanation! So I asked:

"But what about the reports of them bombing Red Cross trains?"

"Well... we can't expect them to abide by the Geneva Convention, if the trains are loaded with ammunition instead of wounded men!"

We stared at him:

This was hard to believe, but somehow we felt that he was speaking the truth.

Then he said:

"We must be on our way. It'll soon be over. The Amis will take care of our men."

They both got up, and we followed them to the door, where the Corporal turned to us and smiled:

" Will you promise me something? All three of you?"

We looked at his kind face, so young and yet so much older than his years. What did he want?

"When the tanks come, don't panic! Stay indoors until they put up their proclamations. Stick to their rules, and you'll be quite safe!"

We promised.

We said good-bye and shook hands. We waved and then stared after them....

Gradually the vehicles were swallowed by the dust of the road. In spite of the reassuring talk, we suddenly felt utterly alone and abandoned...and at the same time there was a feeling of deep sadness:

Two worn-out Ambulances, making their bumpy way out of the village...they seemed symbolic of this end of an era.... A handful of wounded men, representing the once powerful German Army!

It was not long before the next visitor arrived.

There was a knock on the kitchen door, and there stood a man in uniform. He was silhouetted darkly against the bright sunlight in the yard outside, and I suppose we all thought:

"Another soldier."

And we asked him in.

He stepped inside, leaving the door open.

Perhaps we were too pre-occupied with cares about the immediate future, or perhaps we took it for granted that there would be more footsore men arriving to ask for food, drink, or clothes.

When we talked about him afterwards, both the cousins and I agreed that until he sat down on the corner seat, none of us seemed to notice that there was something odd about this one.

He was carrying a rifle with a fixed bayonet....

And I wondered why?

And there was the strange way he was looking at us one minute, and then he seemed to be staring into the distance the next, as if he was listening for something.

He sat with the rifle between his knees.

His face, with a few days' stubble on it, had a sort of unapproachable look; and all our attempts at conversation were answered in monosyllables....

When Hilda handed him a mug of coffee, he drank thirstily, but even while he was drinking, he kept the rifle wedged between his knees. It seemed a strange thing to do. He could quite easily have placed it in the corner next to him!

I remember Martha suggesting this, but he declined.

And as soon as he had given back the empty mug, he placed both hands around the gun and started to twirl it between them, fixing his gaze on it without saying a word.

It was nerve-racking to watch, and I thought:

"Perhaps he's trying to summon up courage to ask for civilian clothes?"

Waiting

Later that day, I discovered that Martha and Hilda had been thinking along the same lines....

And we thanked our lucky stars we hadn't offered him any!

There was a long awkward silence.

I think we were all feeling nervous, faced by that menacing weapon. It kept turning and turning in his restless hands, and in an attempt to break the tension, I remarked casually:

"You soon won't need that any more. Won't it be a relief?"

I can still see him:

He straightened his back, stopped his twirling for a moment and fixed me with a cold stare.

"That time has not come yet!" he said, and his voice had a hollow ring.

None of us felt like talking after that.

But then he suddenly broke the silence. He looked up from the gun and asked Martha:

" Have they delivered any Panzer-Fausts in this village?"

She told him that we'd seen them handed in at the Burgermaster's house that morning.

Now, I knew that both cousins felt as I did: that to hand out these weapons to civilians was either lunacy or a crime! But what ever possessed me to let this unfriendly stranger know how I felt? He hadn't given us the slightest encouragement to even hold a normal conversation, hadn't smiled or said thank-you when Martha had asked him in....

I must have been so sure of our impending deliverance...I threw all caution to the wind and declared recklessly:

"Well, we'll be alright if no-one is mad enough to use the things! What's the point at this hour?"

He turned towards me, his hard eyes staring coldly at my face.

And as he turned, the light from the small kitchen window fell on him... and I saw what we had missed so far:

There were two empty patches on his collar...a small rectangle on each side, where the material was darker, because it had not faded like the rest of his tunic...something had been removed from there...something that he did not want people to see....

He had removed the insignia!

The truth struck me like lightning!

But before my terrified brain could fully grasp its meaning, he spoke,

All Because Of him

this time addressing all three of us:

"In case you think I'm one of the bastards crawling to the enemy to give themselves up - I'm from the Waffen-SS! I'm looking for deserters who have donned civilian clothes. We know they're hiding in these villages. My orders are to shoot them on the spot, as well as the traitors who've helped them!"

Oh God!

He looked at each of us in turn with steely, unblinking eyes.

I wondered if he could have watched the soldiers leave by the back gate? Did he know the truth? Or was he only trying to scare us?

It was impossible to tell.

I sent an extra fast emergency-prayer skywards, for ourselves as well as for our two young soldiers....

They had been right about the Waffen SS! Had this brute already come upon them and done his dirty work?

Then Martha, bless her, managed to tell him as calmly as if she were discussing the day's chores, that there were no men hiding in this house. And she warned:

"You'd best be on your way, because the Americans might get here any minute now!"

Had she touched his Achilles heel?

I was too scared at that moment to realize, that the man was probably on the run himself. If not, why would he remove the symbols, which identified him as an SS-man?

Staring back at him, I now noticed that he had no shoulder straps either!

I decided to add an after-thought to my prayer:

"Please, God, make him get out of here — fast!"

But looking back on it later, I thought that God had done his part already by making Martha say those timely words of warning! It seemed they had prompted the stranger to decide on a hasty exit!

He got up, gripped his rifle tightly in his left hand, raised his right arm, snapped a curt "Heil Hitler" and strutted out of the kitchen....

He didn't notice that none of us returned his salute.

"Pooh," Hilda breathed, "that just goes to show we aren't safe yet! Do you think he suspects anything?"

"I think he was bluffing." Martha said. Her opinnion of the man probably came nearest the truth. She went on:

Waiting

"There was something very strange about him. But I daresay he would shoot any ordinary soldier just to get his uniform!"

Then we sat in silence again and waited.

Another hour or so went by.

Then, from the direction we expected the Allies to enter the village, we heard a strange rattling, like the wheels of iron-rimmed carts on stones....

We looked at each other. This wasn't the noise of tank-engines, but what on earth was it?

Cautiously, we went to the gate and looked up the street. And we saw....

Were our eyes playing a trick?

Or was it a living nightmare, a scene from a painting by Hyronimus Bosch?

Down the sunbaked street came several high two-wheel carts.

They were being pushed by people who were only partially clothed in what looked like pyjamas. But they hardly looked like human beings:

Like living skeletons, with painfully slow steps, they shuffled over the uneven stones. Some of them were hanging on to the long handles and the sides rather than pushing the heavy carts. When they came closer, we saw that what had seemed to be sticks and bundles of loose rags from the distance were people packed tightly on top of the vehicles.

It was impossible to tell who was alive and who was dead.

One of the figures struggling along by the side took the hand of one person, which was dangling down over the edge, and placed it gently onto the chest of the prone figure. It seemed a gesture of such care that I wondered if they might be brothers.

They all looked alike with their shaven heads and deep-sunken eyes, eyes which had no sparkle left in them.

However, that gentle gesture had not gone unnoticed by the barbarians who accompanied this sad procession: About half a dozen SS-men with sub machine guns were shouting and cursing, pushing and prodding at the half-dead prisoners, urging them to move faster....

Now the guard nearest the prisoner I had been watching jumped towards him and hit him with the butt of his gun. The prisoner sank to his knees. He made no sound, not of pain, nor of protest, and I prayed that he was beyond any more pain....

The guard made them stop the cart and told two of the other poor wretches to throw the inert figure onto the others. Then he shouted:

All Because Of Him

...But they hardly looked like human beings...

Waiting

"Get a move on, you devils!"

And they slowly stumbled along and made their way Eastwards out of the village.

I looked at Martha and Hilda. The three of us were weeping silently. And when we went back indoors, we just sat in the kitchen, feeling numb, stunned into silence by what we had just witnessed.

Of course, by the end of the war, we had all heard rumours of places, where people were being kept in dreadful conditions. But how could human beings be brought to this state of living death?

Not long after that, we heard the sound of gunfire, sharp, rattly sounds like those of machine guns. Again we knew that it couldn't be the Allies, because it came from the East... maybe not more than a mile or so away from us.... We guessed it could be no further than the nearest hamlet, and it came from the direction the doomed prisoners had taken....

Soon all was quiet again.

But the ensuing silence became even more menacing. I think each of us had the same awful suspicion. And we all rejected it:

Things like that just could not happen in our country! Or could they?

Then, all of a sudden, there was the thunderous rumble of tanks at the top of the street, making Hilda jump and race upstairs to put out the sheet.

Martha and I followed hard on her heels: Even if we kept to the advice from our young Corporal to stay indoors, we had to see what was going to happen next!

So once our flag of truce was fixed safely, we squeezed into the opening of the attic window; and as we looked down, the street became filled with people, especially children. They had managed to wriggle out of the grip of their elders, and now they were close to the tanks, heedless of possible danger.

But there was no danger!

Glancing up at the other houses, we saw white sheets everywhere.

And the American soldiers would have seen them before they passed the first fences; they would know that we'd all had enough by now! It had probably been the same in all the other villages through which they had passed during the day.

And so they rolled in.

Just two tanks with their turrets open, and sun tanned soldiers reaching down to the village children, handing them chocolates and sweets!

All Because Of Him

Even the young women, who had joined the urchins, didn't go empty: A shower of nylon stockings rained down on them from the passing vehicles!

Watching the spectacle from on high, the three of us were crying and laughing all at the same time.

It was all so simple and yet so different from what we had expected. There was no high drama, just more and more people coming out from their houses, some of them waving, children laughing and shouting in their scramble for the unheard of treasures!

And above it all the sun shone, and I felt like shouting with the rest of them, because the relief was so great!

Yet at the same time there was this mournful feeling, which kept welling up inside me. For the second time that day, I was reminded of 'Gone With The Wind': The thought of all the lives lost on both sides — and for what?

And there was also the knowledge that this was only the beginning of the end! In many parts of the country there would still be more fighting and more senseless dying....

But at the same time one part of me was full of hope. I thought that surely at the end of all this, mankind would learn to live in peace?

I was young. At twenty-one it was still possible to believe that people would learn from history!

After watching for a while, when we were quite sure that it was safe to go outside, Martha,Hilda and I decided we'd have a closer look. The tanks had by now pulled into the large open yard opposite us, and some of the American Soldiers had jumped down.

Their Officer gave some orders, after which one soldier walked to the barn door and put up a large poster. It gave details about curfew and the handing in of any weapons etc. (They even demanded the handing in of cameras! But I reckoned that was for personal perks....).

And throughout all this there was no hint of open animosity: The villagers stood around, marvelling at the size of the tanks. Children lingered, with their mouths still drooling from the chocolates, perhaps hoping there might be more....

Polish prisoners, too, came on the scene. They made sure, though, to stand a little way apart from us Germans, to show that they were different!

As we walked across the road I wondered about the Burgermaster. But he was nowhere to be seen. Just as well!

Waiting

Then there was a happy surprise. Someone was shouting at us. The voice came from one of the broad shelves on the rear of the tanks:

"Hello! We've made it!"

And there sat our two young soldiers, our first visitors of the day! They were back in their uniforms, and judging by the look on their faces, they were right as rain. I asked:

"How was it?"

"O.K.,"the first one said. "They just ordered us to climb onto the tanks, and then they gave us some fags!"

And the second one, smiling down on us, laughed:

"You'll never believe what their Captain said, when I asked him what would happen to us. He said they would need us to push the Red Army out of Germany!"

Well, it was obvious that I wasn't the only person full of hope, given to dreams of euphoria! If the Americans felt that they'd manage that, why shouldn't I keep hoping for a miracle?

Oh, there would be such rejoicing, once we were all really free!

I even caught myself thinking of venturing across the Elbe in search of my mother! Even though I had never felt as close to her as to my father, I wanted to know she was safe!

At the time none of us were aware that within a very short time from now the bridges across the river Elbe were going to be blown up, reputedly by the SS.... And after that, the Allies would stare across the broad waters at each other, until British soldiers, who took over the region to begin with, built a wooden bridge. It would not be open to the general public until much later in the summer.

But all that was yet to come.

For the moment, everybody relished the thought that the village had had a happy release! Some of the farmers went back into their houses to collect their guns: There would be no rabbit shooting for the time being! They realized that it would be no use hiding the weapons....

There were going to be house-to-house searches.

The Burgermaster's farm was one of the first places to be entered. And there they discovered and took away the Panzer-Fausts. The Burgermaster himself was said to be somewhere in hiding....

Later still, it was said he'd disappeared....We wondered: "Rough Justice?" We couldn't blame the Poles.

All Because Of Him

After the Americans had finished the searches, the Captain gave orders to move on, and they left for the next village.

We waved to our two happy soldiers and went back indoors, where we flopped down on the bench, and Martha sighed:

"What a day it's been!"

Then, ever the practical housewife, she made some more coffee.

But before night-fall, we were to hear of a sequel to the drama we had witnessed that afternoon. The last act had been staged just outside the nearest hamlet....

It was one of the Poles who came to tell us of it.

Apparently the Americans had come upon a hastily covered shallow mass-grave. The emaciated corpses had been dumped in a hollow under a tree, loosely spread over with soil and branches.

The Tank Commanders had threatened to raze the adjacent village to the ground, unless the inhabitants revealed the culprits....

Then one of the Poles had come forward. He had explained, with many gestures and a few words of broken English, how some of the Poles had watched the massacre from the distance:

When the SS-men had realized that they weren't able to move any further, they had murdered all the ones who were still alive of that tragic group of people.

So the village was spared, thanks to the Poles.

And thus the day ended on a sad note. I'd had no part in the tragedy. But I had seen the victims struggle along to their doom, and I felt ashamed of my country.

My parents c.1940.

That's me aged $2^1/_2$ ...and my first day at school.

Photo for Dad's birthday
October 1933.

...the year HE came to power!

Taken from the balcony that
fell down 3 floors—Spring 1941
a few months before Jutta's death.

Harald Caspers,
Teacher and friend.

98b

The Vicarage, after some trees had been pruned.
The left gable-end was Peter's escape route.

The Vicarage from the garden.
Uncle Fred and a grandchild c.1947.

Early days with Karl
- Spring 1941.

My family -
Winter 1941.

Autumn 1948 - after leaving
the Eastern Sector

...and today.

Across The River

Summer 1945. It was some weeks after Magdeburg had been handed over to the Red Army. I stood in the queue outside the tall office block, where the Russian Commander held sway. The queue grow longer every minute. After arriving there at the crack of dawn, I was now waiting with many others, for a pass to cross to the other side of the river Elbe. Apparently, one had to see someone called the 'Commandant', even though no-one knew how high or low this official might rank in real terms....

There had been rumours that the bridge would be open from today. But there had been rumours many times before...and each time the waiting had ended in disappointment for everyone, including myself!

Would it be different today, so I could begin my search?

It was months since I had last seen my parents.

After we had lost the flat, my father had taken Mother to stay with her sister beyond the Elbe. He just couldn't believe that the Russians would go further than Berlin! He himself had returned to his place of work in Hanover, intending to live in the cellar beneath his office.

And while Mother had been caught up in the first onslaught of the victorious Red Army flooding the country to the East of the Elbe, I had been staying with some of my husband's relatives. They hadn't suffered any war-damage, and most of them seemed to look on me as a cross between a poor church mouse and a modern Cinderella!

It had been quite hard to accept being a poor relation....

As soon as it was safe to move into Magdeburg I'd gone to stay with my husband's parents there, until civilians would be allowed to cross to the

All Because Of Him

East of the river....But Karl's parents didn't seem to understand that it was imperative for me to know what had happened to my mother. They kept up a continuous flow of bickering on the subject.

It was becoming intolerable.

And now, while I was waiting to get that pass, I was hoping it wouldn't be in vain this time. I remembered the sneering face of my mother-in-law on the last occasion, when I had returned empty handed. Her husband had sat at the kitchen table, supporting his wife's biting remarks with slow grumbles, saying that there was no need for me to go traipsing about the countryside. Hadn't I got all I could wish for?

Last night, too, there had been an ugly scene, after I'd told them that I would leave as soon as it got light, to join the queue outside the Russian Headquarters.

SHE had said:

"I call it a wild goose-chase!"

"But can't you see? I MUST go and see what's happened to my mother!"

But she still kept on and on about there being no call to leave them to go on that kind of jaunt....

"After all, You've got US!"

"Lord give me strength!" I had thought and told her that there was no point trying to talk me out of going.

"What if the boy comes home when you're away?"

She thought that this would 'bring me to my senses'!

But I always found it irritating, when she referred to her son as 'the boy'...after all he was thirty-two years old!

I had found myself running out of patience and said that one's own mother was different from a mother in law... and that Karl knew where Uncle Fred's vicarage was because he'd been there before!

"He can find me there the same as here!" I had ended.

"Let her go!" The old man had growled: "All she can think of is gallivanting!"

It had seemed best to leave the room; and I turned away from both of them, heaving an angry sigh...which made Mother-in-law lose her temper altogether:

She was making a stew, stirring the contents of a large saucepan, holding its lid in her left hand... and she threw the lid at me!

I didn't know whether she had aimed badly, or whether it was because she'd used her left hand...anyway, she missed! I was quite nimble in those days, which may have helped. But something inside me snapped, and I suddenly burst out laughing....

Angry laughter, and they didn't speak to me after that.

So early this morning, I'd picked up my bag and left without a word. It would no doubt be one of the first things they would tell Karl, IF he came back....

And now I was waiting in this ever growing queue, wondering if the doors would open eventually. I looked at my watch: Eight o'clock!

Suddenly there came an audible sigh from the crowd!

The tall doors swung open, and two soldiers placed themselves by either of its posts. One of them stepped forward holding up both hands and, showing all five fingers on each, he called:

"Come!"

The first ten in the crowd moved up the few steps to the entrance, where the guards counted them, let them pass, and then placed themselves squarely in the open space to bar anyone's attempt at jumping the queue.

I had been number eleven, so I now had a good view as, at short intervals, one after the other of the the ten reappeared. Studying their faces, I could tell the ones who'd been successful and got their pass, and those who'd failed, because for some reason or other, the Commandant had not seen fit to let them have the vital piece of paper.

So the hopes of the people waiting in the long line rose and fell with each man or woman emerging from the lion's den, depending on whether they were smiling or not as they came out....

At last the soldier held up another ten fingers, and I led the next lot up the steps, was duly counted, and then ushered into a large office, where the Commandant sat behind an enormous desk. He wore a bemedalled uniform, and it was plain to see how important he felt: It was the way he stuck out his glittering chest, bringing his double chins to rest one on top of another.

He stared at me for a few seconds and then said something in Russian to a young man standing next to him. Until that moment I hadn't really looked at that one. He was wearing civilian clothes, and his face hardly had any colour; but when he noticed my eyes resting on him, he smiled at me... and I thought:

"Where have I seen his face before?"

For the moment I could not place it.... His smile stayed with me, though, and gave me a glimmer of hope.

The boss turned to me now, and the young man began to translate his questions. To begin with, it was quite straightforward:

Name, age, profession, (if any), present address...all quite easy. So far the fat man appeared satisfied. He kept nodding like a Buddha, pressing and releasing the various chins every time my answers were translated to him.

But then came the tricky bit! And if it hadn't been for the strange young man's help, I would have been one of the sad-faced people, making my way out of the building, without hope of getting across the river for maybe months to come!

The question had been:

"What is your reason for wanting to get a pass?"

I began by stating that my mother was on the other side of the Elbe... and I was going to add that I wished to find out if she was still alive... but by sheer good luck I caught the expression on the translator's face.

He was not smiling now but seemed to be trying to convey a kind of message to me: His eyes, under slightly lowered brows, never left my face, and he now pressed his lips tightly together, while at the same time he gave the minutest shake of his head....

Did he want me to keep quiet?

But before I could figure out what he meant, and before the Commandant had a chance to read my bewilderment, the translator said:

"You want to go to the place where you were born. Please state the name of that place!"

"Oh, but I wasn't..." I stammered, but he quickly interrupted, saying again that I wished to return to my birthplace, and before I could utter another word, he translated it for the Commandant.

And now the fat man leaned forward, picked up a pen and wrote down something on one of the forms lying in front of him....

While he was writing, with his eyes fixed on the document, I gazed at the young man....

I KNEW I'd seen him before, but where?

It couldn't have been very long ago either, because I could feel the memory of meeting him bubbling just beneath the surface... and while the Commandant was still scribbling away, breathing heavily with the effort, it suddenly came to me:

In an instant I was back outside the farm house, where I had been staying with Karl's aunt and uncle. It must have been late in April or perhaps early May. Some time after the Americans had rolled in, or soon after the British Army had taken over the district West of Magdeburg....

It had been unusually warm for the time of year, and one day a man, who looked more like a skeleton than a human being, had come to the farm gate.

Across The River

I saw him lean heavily against one of the posts. He was dirty and dishevelled, and it was impossible to guess at his age. His clothes were in tatters, and the sleeves of his threadbare jacket left his wrists exposed half way up to his elbows....

It was those wrists which made me dash out to him to offer my help: Festering sores where circling both of them like painful bracelets! I had seen sores like these several times since the end of the war. Some of the prisoners released from the Death-Camps bore the same marks: they had been caused by wearing shackles....

I had gone out and told him to wait, while I got some Iodine and pieces of linen to clean and bandage his sores.

All the time I had worked on his wrists, he had kept his face averted, probably wanting to hide the pain. After I'd finished, I offered him food and coffee, but he declined, saying he wanted to move on, to see if his mother was still alive....

"She lives near Helmstedt," he had said, "and I haven't seen her since they took me away! She thinks I'm dead!"

And then he had told me that just before the end of the war, he and the other prisoners had been made to write a letter telling their people that by the time they got the message. the writer would be dead!

I had stared at him, thinking of the parents, wives, brothers and children who had received letters like that....

"My mother will think I'm a ghost, when I arrive on her doorstep!" He had added, and I had thought that anyone could be forgiven, for taking him for a ghost, with his deep-sunken eyes, the shaven head, and the bony frame....

And then he'd asked, if he could just have a drink of water.

So I had filled a big tumbler with cool water from the creaking old pump in the yard. It was after he had drunk it that he gave me the warm smile, which had remained in my memory....

Could this man be that Ex-Prisoner?

It was the smile, which had brought it all back, even though he looked a different person now:

No hollow cheeks, and his bluey-grey eyes no longer deeply embedded inside the shaven skull!

My reminiscences were interrupted by the fat man raising his head from his strenuous job. He said something in Russian, and then handed the finished certificate to the translator.

The latter read it, first to himself, and then aloud to me. And I realized that he was 'translating' more than the mere statement written by his boss:

"It says here, that you are returning to Gertern, where your home is, and where you were born!"

I nodded silently, even though I couldn't see why it had to say something which was nowhere near the truth, and he explained, still looking at the piece of paper, as if he were reading from it:

"Unless you'd said THAT, you would have been turned down! That was why I had to stop you...you might have said the wrong thing!"

"I'm sorry," I said, and he smiled again....And this time I was sure he was that prisoner! He now handed me the form and added:

"Luckily, my boss really doesn't understand any German at all! So I told him I knew you as a child in your village!"

He said something in Russian to the Commandant, who gave a sort of grunt, like agreeing to something; and the young man started to lead me to the exit....

"I've told him I'll walk you to the front door, because I'm a friend of your family!"

"Won't he mind?"

"No, Ex-Concentration Camp Prisoners get privileged treatment; and, as Russians go, this one isn't a bad boss!"

"How did you come to be a translator?"

"Oh, my mother's people were Russian Exiles. And during the war someone overheard us talk in Russian: After that I was considered a security risk! Hence the Camp!"

"And now you were taking a risk to get me my pass...why?"

There was a pause....

We had reached the top of the steps outside the building, and now, for the last time, he smiled at me and said:

"I'll never forget how YOU helped ME!"

And then he went back indoors to the fat man's office, while I slowly went down the steps, thinking how the wheel of life had turned....

But there was no time to lose now. I had to get ready for the long walk across the Elbe and beyond!

When I returned to the flat, mother-in-law greeted me with the smirk I had expected.

But I just waved the pass at her and packed a few belongings into my homemade rucksack.

And then I was off!

Across The River

She hadn't even asked if I wanted a bottle of water for the journey... but what did it matter? I could get water from the farmers by the roadside. It was July, harvest time...there would be people working in the fields somewhere....

So I started walking.

Stepping out briskly to begin with, I first had to pass through the ravaged centre of the city, before I got to the wooden bridge. It was a temporary replacement. The British Engineers had built it before the Red Army took over the city.

I walked across the new structure. The remnants of the old bridge lay accusingly half in and half out of the water. I had been told by an eye witness that the SS had blown it up at the last minute. According to that man's gruelling description, those SS men had blown up a farmer and his wagon and horses, despite his entreaties to wait till he'd got to the other side!

By the time I went across, the waters had washed away the sad remains.

The Russian guards at the turnpike gave my pass a quick glance, but then stared rather rudely at my figure, before deciding to let me walk on!

I was hoping it wasn't a foretaste of the attitudes of the many other soldiers I might come across during the next few hours... because I'd heard there were Russian quarters in several places along that road.

But it was a fine day, and it was pleasant walking...first by a stretch of the river, and then along an avenue, shaded by trees. I thought how good it felt, knowing that every step was taking me further away from Karl's parents and everlasting nagging.

"And not a Russian soldier in sight!" I told myself.

Well, of course, I shouldn't have said that, even though there was no-one there to hear me say it!

Because, a minute or so after, there came the sound of clip-clopping hooves; and from the rattling noise following it, I knew it must be one of those trough-like, low wagons the Russians used for carrying personnel, transporting provisions and removing confiscated property....

Clip-clop, clip-clop, and then clip...clop...clip...clop...they were slowing down as they came closer. It would be useless to try and outpace them: I couldn't compete with one of their sturdy, unkempt, pony-sized horses, and the soldiers would take it as a sign of fear, which would ensure disaster from the start.

So far, I had kept looking straight ahead, in spite of the temptation to turn around: I wanted to know how many men were on that cart! When they drew level with me, I counted seven.

All Because Of Him

One of them was an Officer, and, in my ignorance, I thought that made it less dangerous!

So I kept on walking, accompanied by their funny little contraption....

But then they started talking to me, in their kind of broken German, asking me where I was going, and did I want a lift....

What should I do?

At first I tried ignoring them, hoping they would soon get tired of the one-sided dialogue... but no, they persisted, and I realized that the Officer was doing most of the talking!

If I couldn't get rid of them, maybe I should try and talk my way out of it?

And so, the next time one of them patted the straw on the wagon with his hand, like asking a dog to jump up, I said:

"No thank you ! I can walk!"

But having once responded to their pestering, there was no stopping them: Where was I going? Why didn't I want to join them? Wouldn't I like just a short ride to have a rest?

It was useless trying to put them off!

And so far I had not detected anything in their manner which might suggest an ulterior motive.... On the other hand, their attitude was bound to change if I made them angry.

The Officer now said:

"We go station, you go station?"

I shook my head:

"No, I go other village...station is left. I turn right!"

"O.K.,you come on wagon! See sign-post, you say stop! We stop!"

It seemed there was no way out, so I nodded, and they stopped the pony. I hoisted myself up by the side of the cart, and off we went....

As soon as I had settled on the straw, one of the soldiers put his hand on the top of my rucksack and asked:

"Is heavy? Take off?"

"No thank you, is alright!" I wasn't going to take unnecessary risks with my few belongings or with my person! Keeping on the rucksack provided me with a sort of armour-plated rear! It was not a very good fit and came down as far as my buttocks.

It wasn't very comfortable, when I was walking, but now it seemed ideal!

He took his hand away. And they started chatting with each other, interrupted by occasional laughter....It made me feel they were really not much

106

more than mischievious boys, looked at from where I was sitting.

I was beginning to feel quite comfortable there on the straw, with the clip-clop of the little horse trotting along at an even pace, my back resting against my rucksack. On the other side of it sat one of the young men, leaning against it as well, sort of balancing things out. There was no more attempt at relieving me of my load, and all was well... or so I thought....

It wasn't until, some time later, when I stopped to shorten the shoulder straps, that I noticed they had pinched my pullover! It was the only warm piece of clothing I owned at that time, and I had strapped it to the top of the rucksack in case the evening turned out cool. It would be easily accessible there: But obviously, someone else had thought so, too!

Still, I thought if that was all, as far as any mishaps were concerned during the trip, I mustn't really grumble....

However, while I was still on the cart, I thought these were really nice lads!

After a couple of miles, I saw the sign post which pointed to the station: I had to get off! I asked the Officer to stop, and to my relief and surprise, he gave a command to the soldier holding the reins. The soldier said something to the little horse, and the horse came to a standstill....

"What a decent fellow!" I thought, (meaning the Officer), as I slid down from the cart....

I smiled a sort of all-around smile, including men and Officer alike, saying thank-you and good-bye... when the latter jumped off the wagon, walked up to me and asked:

"You married?"

"Yes."

"Where husband?"

I shrugged my shoulders and said:

"Don't know...away somewhere."

"Husband soldier?"

I nodded.

He smiled; it was really quite a friendly smile, when I thought of it later.(like most of the Russians I've met, he had brilliant white teeth!) And he said:

"Me soldier too! I be your husband! Half hour I your husband in woods, yes?"

A quick glance around me showed that the fork in the road was flanked by woods on all sides, and I thought:

"I mustn't let him see that he's scared me!"

I told myself to keep smiling, keep calm and pretend I was neither shocked nor angered, nor anything else. I told him:

"No, going to find Mamushka, get too late! No time for woods now!"

He seemed disappointed, but he was still smiling, when he took my hand and said:

"You go find Mamushka!"

And with that he went back to his seat. The soldier flicked the reins and told the horse to move on, and they all gave a friendly wave, as the wagon started rolling....

I stood and waved, till they were out of sight!

Then I walked on. It was getting close to midday, and I was glad of the trees alongside the road. It seemed deserted, but I didn't mind. Even as a child, I had loved exploring and roving about on my own.

And as I made my way, I thought of the gentlemanly Officer, and how lucky I'd been, to meet someone like him and not one of the terrors of the countryside, the ones who were said to go about raping and plundering even now!

Ignorance is bliss, and so I even found myself wondering, if these tales had any truth in them at all...seeing how easy it had been to take my leave....

As the sun got hotter, I found myself thinking of the uncle's vicarage with its thick ancient walls which kept out heat and cold alike.

Pictures of my mother, the aunt and uncle, the various cousins and their children floated like mirages through my mind. I imagined them sitting in the shade of one the old trees outside the kitchen, sipping ice-cold lemon-juice!

Oh, stop daydreaming: Where would anyone get a lemon in the Eastern Sector!

After walking for another hour or so, I saw some movement under the trees a little way ahead.

Maybe farm workers having a rest?

I would ask them for a drink!

But I had only gone another few yards, when a turnpike came down across the road, and two soldiers stepped out from under the trees, putting up a hand as a signal to stop.

I stopped and one of them said:

"Paper!" Just the one word.

I fished out the pass from inside my shoulder bag, held it out to him and watched as his slanted eyes glanced at the flimsy piece of paper. He was deeply tanned,and his face was full of pock marks; I thought he must be from the far Eastern parts of the Soviet Union, perhaps from somewhere in Mongolia....

Across The River

The way he was holding my pass seemed strangely deferential, and then I realized he was holding it upside down! So he couldn't read! That would explain the awe with which he treated this vital document of mine!

After a few seconds, his mate stepped close to him and had a look as well. He nodded, and the little pock-marked one said:

"Is good!" And handed back my pass.

"Thank you," I said, and they raised the bar and let me go on my way....

I thought that by now a quick "Thank-you-God" was in order!

It really had been so easy to get past the Russians I'd met so far!

And on I went, now passing through a large forested area, feeling light-hearted and ready to face the next encounter....

The forest was interspersed with vast stretches of heathland and copses of birch trees, but was completely void of human habitation.

At the end of the woods, however, there would be fields stretching for miles on either side.... There would be people working in them somewhere, and somehow that thought was comforting....

By now I was so hot, sweat was making my cotton dress cling to my back, and bits of grit and dust between my toes were digging into the skin.

"I should have taken my calf length boots!" I thought.

But they were the my only good pair of footwear... I had worn them on the day of the fires in March, when I'd gone to see Karl off at the barracks. That's why they hadn't been lost when everything else went up in smoke, and since then I had treated them as a prized treasure. Leather shoes were as rare as gold dust, and I wouldn't dream of wearing them in the summer!

Instead I had donned a pair of hand-me-down sandals, but they were split at the front, and every bit of grit seemed to find its way into that gap!

On and on I trudged.

There seemed to be no end of of alder and pines, and here and there the arrays of slender birches. Their delicate branches hardly moved in the still air. Even the trees seemed stifled in this heat.

After I passed across a hot stretch of bare heath with no shade whatsoever, I came to yet another copse of birches.

"I must be nearing the end of the woods," I thought, remembering a picnic we'd had there in the past....

Then I heard voices in the distance, and there was the welcome sound of human laughter.

But only a little further on, it became clear that they were not the voices of farm workers!

No, the people taking their ease under the Birches were Russians, ten of them! And now I saw to my dismay that there were bottles lying around in the grass, full ones and empties....

As I came closer, one of them lifted a bottle from his lips and waved it about in the air, shouting:

"Stoy!" The Russian word for 'Stop'...

I stopped, keeping a few feet away from the tree where he and his comrades lay. They looked a mottled crowd and had a decidedly bedraggled look about them.

And I could smell the drink from where I stood!

Once again, I thought:

"Keep calm, smile! Don't antagonise them!"

To begin with, though, I just stood there, sort of waiting for the first move in a game. Then the one who had told me to stop said something to the others over his shoulder...and they all laughed!

I thought he was probably their leader....

It was plain to see that they were all drunk, ranging from rather merry to downright befuddled and worse! And they were obviously not a patrol on duty....

And again, I felt they were so young! What if I think of them as rowdy school boys, unruly, insolent, excitable, but just boys!

And like me: They were a long way from home, perhaps missing their own mothers.... I wondered, if I could get away THIS time by telling them of my search for 'Mamushka'?

Of course, this lot were different altogether from the Officer and his men on the little cart...but it might work, and if it didn't, what choice had I got anyway?

The spokesman now asked:

"Where you go?"

His words revealed that he was sort of lazily drunk, but again, there appeared to be no threat in his manner. So I decided not to mention about Mother just yet, and said guardedly:

"Next village, Gertern."

Did I imagine it, or did the mention of that village stir something at the back of his mind? He narrowed his eyes, cocked his head and asked:

"Why?"

Oh, well, I'd better tell him!

"Find old Mamushka!"

...I could smell the drink from where I stood...

All Because Of Him

He eyed me up and down, as if he was debating whether to let me go or not — My mouth was as dry as the sandy soil beneath my feet — Then he smiled drunkenly and said:

"Go later! Half hour with me first! Yes?"

Heavens above! They really didn't seem to have anything else to think about: Vodka and women!

And yet the way they were lolling about under the trees seemed to lack urgency... maybe they were too hot or too tired to make an effort! Even the leader's questions had been put to me in the same way as if a friend asked for a game of tennis, or a stroll along the promenade!

So I answered in the same tone I'd used earlier on, when I'd declined the woodland walk with the Officer... using the same words, and ending with a friendly smile, as if I was truly sorry I couldn't oblige....

He grinned, and again he said something to the others across his shoulder. And again they all laughed, as he swung his near empty bottle towards me:

"Alright! You go find Mamushka!"

I turned away and carried on walking.

They were shouting and laughing, but somehow it didn't worry me any longer. It was obvious that they'd soon all be dead to the world, sleeping it off under the trees....

Even so, it was probably lucky I didn't understand Russian!

Now it was only about three miles more to the village.

The woods were thinning on both sides now. Soon I was passing the last few pines on my left, and then the land lay open and flat for miles, as far as the eye could see. Only the apple trees lining the roadsides were taller than me in all that flatness!

This was the last lap of the trek. The sun on my back was still hot, but a slight haze near the horizon foretold the coming dusk.

Most of the fields here had been harvested already. But after a while, I could see figures moving about among corn stooks. They were loading sheaves of corn onto large farm wagons.

And beyond the fields, though still quite a long way off, there was the tower of my uncle's church, surrounded by trees....

With any luck, I would be there before dark.

But first I must ask those people for some water. When I came close enough, it was a relief to hear them talking in my own language; and by the time I reached the first wagon, they were sitting down, having a break.

Across The River

I walked across the stubble, all sweaty and dishevelled, and every one of them turned and stared at me. One of the women said:

"Where in God's name have you sprung from?"

And when I told them, they looked at each other as if they couldn't believe it! Then an elderly man said:

"You shouldn't have come all that way on your own!"

Too tired to answer, I only shrugged my shoulders and said:

"Please, can I have something to drink!"

There was an old milk churn standing in the shade of a stook, and a man sitting by it dipped his enamel mug and filled it for me with cool water.

He asked if I'd like to sit and eat with them.

I took the water gratefully, but was too weary by now to feel hungry. I told him that I shouldn't be able to get up again, once I'd sat down!

"Pity you're not going our way," he said, "you could have had a ride on the wagon."

I thanked him, handed back his empty mug and went on my way.

Nearer and nearer with each step...my mind racing ahead of me.

I thought I should have asked those people, if they knew what had happened at the vicarage!

But, deep down, I knew why I hadn't done so:

If it was bad news, I didn't wish to hear it from strangers.

I wanted to wait till I got there and find out for myself.

At last there were the first cottages, looking just as I remembered them, whitewashed, red-roofed, fronted by straggling gardens. I thought the people who owned them were either too busy to tend them, or maybe they'd lost heart....

And suddenly, after I had walked past several garden gates, I was struck by the silence....

There was no-one about anywhere!

I entered the street leading to the centre of the village.

All the wooden shutters outside the windows were closed. And with each house I passed, my heart seemed to beat a little faster, till I could hear it like a drum pounding in my ears.

Life in the Eastern Sector was supposed to be getting back to normal... so where were all the people?

I came to the church, surrounded by its ring of Lime trees. The Village Green was deserted.

All Because Of Him

Then I stood outside the vicarage.

It was several hundred years old.

Its shutters were sturdily made by craftsmen of bygone days... and they were closed like all the others.

There was no sound from inside, or from the garden, which lay beyond high walls surrounding the house.

Yet I knew that my uncle and aunt had taken in refugees from all over the place, among them were several young mothers with babies and toddlers....

There should have been the sound of children playing....

Where were the children?

But staring at the silent facade wouldn't do any good. So I rang the bell. It was probably as old as the vicarage itself, and its jangle was enough to startle the deaf!

But even the bell didn't produce any sign of life from inside!

I knocked, and then I hammered on the thick oak door:

Nothing!

I put my ear against it....

And there was a sound of feet shuffling about in the hall... so I shouted my name through the keyhole!

Now I could hear voices in quick surprised discussion; but it took still a few more seconds before the people inside dared trust their ears, dared to believe it was really me!

Then someone drew back the heavy bolts. I heard the key turn in the lock, and the door opened...but only just wide enough to admit the wanderer. An arm reached out and pulled me inside... it belonged to my Uncle Fred.

And once I was in, he hastily locked and bolted the door again as before....

I believe at that first moment I was as stunned, as the people facing me!

But they weren't just surprised — it was more a sort of consternation I read on their faces. And the way they were all huddled together reminded me of a frightened flock of sheep, almost too scared to move....

Then from the midst of them stepped the person I'd come all this way to find:

My mother.

It looked as though she couldn't take it in to begin with... and I noticed how frail she'd become; but after I'd hugged her to me, she kept stroking my arm, as if to make sure I was real.

Across The River

Then suddenly they all spoke at once, wanted to know how I had managed to get there.... Was I alright? Didn't I know how dangerous that stretch of road was even now?

And in between I was being hugged and kissed, and held at arms' length to be looked at.

Actually, I must have looked a sight, with my hair stuck to me, sweat and dust in streaks all over my face, and when someone helped me off with the rucksack, it was found to be soaking wet, right into the middle of the clothes I'd packed!

It seemed no-one minded how messy I looked, and it felt good to be welcomed like this, but I couldn't understand why they were all so astonished to see me alive and undamaged!

Someone handed me some water, and in between sips I told the assembled family all about the trip.

Yet even while I was talking to them, I sensed that their feeling of relief was mixed with some kind of disapproval....

I couldn't help asking WHY they were all so astonished? And why was the village so deadly quiet? Was everyone hiding behind closed shutters like they were in here?

It seemed I had a great deal to learn:

Because after my last question, there was complete silence!

After what seemed ages, when I turned to my Uncle Fred for an answer, he looked at me over his spectacles and said:

"My dear child, you don't know how lucky you've been!"

I just stood there, still waiting for an explanation.

And then he told me:

"Yesterday, a gang of ten drunken Russians raped a girl right here outside the vicarage, on the Village Green!"

Someone stepped forward and took away my empty glass, because all of a sudden my hand was shaking:

There had been ten men in that drinking party....

For A Scrap Of Paper

AUGUST 1945, and almost a month since I'd arrived at Uncle Fred's vicarage. It had been such a relief to find all the inhabitants including my mother still alive.

They had weathered the storm of the incoming Red Army, had survived the house to house searches and the plundering, and physically they hadn't been harmed, but they were all still extremely wary of going out into the streets... because, every now and then, the Russian soldiers were still raping young women wherever they happened to seize them....

However, it was becoming less frequent...and by now there were less suicides.

The old vicarage was full to the brim with old, young and very young people, all trying to live amicably together, all hoping that one day they might return to the places they'd come from....

There were relatives from various parts of Germany, Austria and Czechoslovakia. I'd never met some of them before I arrived in my search for my mother.

She and I had two tiny adjoining rooms in one gable end of the attic; while my cousin Peter, his wife Margo, their two small sons, and Margo's widowed mother lived at the opposite end, all in one huge room. Because of what happened later, I must mention that Margo's mother was half blind and rather frail.

Downstairs there were, apart from my uncle and aunt, various daughters and cousins with their offspring; all living there, because they had nowhere else to go.

On the whole, life went on quietly most of the time.

But every so often we would be hurtled into a panic by orders from the powerful new authority in our lives:

An edict from the Russian Commandant.

He lived in the Manor House a little way along the street; and from there he would issue his edicts, when it suited him....

A poster would appear on the notice board outside the small village shop. It would inform us that all men of a certain age had to assemble outside the Manor House and do a day's work for the Red Army...and with any luck, it might just mean what it said there....

But on several occasions the work force had returned with one or more men missing from their number...and some of those missing were never seen again!

But in spite of these and other upheavals, we were attempting to conduct our lives as normally as possible.

Then one fine morning in August, there appeared yet another order from on high: Every household had to send several ablebodied members, men as well as women, to a forest a few miles away. There they were to cut and clear away charred timber in the burnt out section in the centre.

Since there were quite a few old people living in the vicarage, and since nursing mothers and children were exempt, the task fell to Peter, Margo and myself. Margo said:

"I wonder what the catch is, this time?"

"I can't see a catch in this one," declared Peter, "seeing that we are even allowed to take away all the wood for our own use!"

"How are we going to get the logs home?" I asked.

"Oh, I've asked the farmer I work for. He'll let us borrow his wagon and the horses on the second day out. The first day we'll have to do all the sawing and cutting...and I'll ask for the loan of the old grandfather as well!"

Both Margo and I laughed, but Peter was quite serious:

"I mean it! The old man likes to play an active part once in a while; he can take home the first load, while we are having a rest at lunch time...he'll enjoy a day with his old pals!"

"What old pals?" Margo asked, and he told her that he meant the old horses, of course, who were almost as old as the old man:

"That's if you reckon in horse's years!"

All Because Of Him

So we were all set.

During the first day we hacked and sawed. It was hard work, not least because we had to be extra careful, since none of the people working with us in the fire-blackened forest, had much knowledge of felling trees.

That particular stand had contained only immature trees; but even so, we all shouted 'Timber' long before we heard the creaking of the splintering trunks, just to be on the safe side....

We worked all day with a short break for lunch, and by the time we set out for home, we were looking like seasoned charcoal burners, covered in soot!

The next day dawned...promising a true, golden summer's day. There was no hint of anything untoward to happen.

The old farmer arrived just after sunrise. It would take time for the horses to get to the woods; and we wanted to get the first load on the way before having a rest in the midday heat. Peter climbed onto the front seat with the old man, while Margo and I sat in the back of the cart, with the basket containing our lunch between us. She was in high spirits:

"I think today will be easier. I mean, loading can't be as hard as all the bending and twisting when we were sawing!"

"Don't forget, the logs are heavy!" Peter warned, speaking over his shoulder, "we've got to get them across the ruts, because the horses can get the wagon only as far as the fire-break ditch."

But Margo was undaunted, saying she was sure that we'd get all the wood home in two loads, adding:

"And afterwards, we'll have a dip in the pond...just think how lovely and cool it'll be!"

And during that morning all three of us would remind each other of the vision of the deep cool pond in the vicarage garden... with the overhanging beech trees filtering golden sun-specks onto the water....

But we were all wrong.

The day turned out to be very different, though none of us had the slightest inkling of it, as we arrived at the clearing.

Some of the other people were already busy at work, and we lost no time in starting to load, while the old man was taking it easy. He was sitting propped against a wheel of his cart, smoking a pipe.

Oh, but it was hot! Soon the sun was burning down on our backs, and once in a while we would straighten up, wipe the sweat from our grimy faces and glance at the progress of our fellow workers.

"Just look at some of their contraptions!" Margo whispered,"how on earth are they going to drag them home?"

"Well, just think yourself lucky that I've got friends in high places!" Peter whispered back, grinning and then nodding in the direction of the old farmer, who was by now fast asleep in the shade of his wagon....

Margo laughed:

"I wouldn't fancy pushing any of this home in our old pram!"

And sure enough, that was what quite a number of people were using to get their share of the wood to their homes in or around our village. It would mean going to and fro all day long for some of them, and I felt sorry for their plight.

A few luckier ones were loading their logs onto sturdy fourwheeled hand carts, such as were common in the German countryside at the time. But the majority were manhandling unwieldy pieces of wood onto rickety makeshift affairs, built with sets of old pram and pushchair wheels.

Our own logs were beginning to pile up on the wagon.

It stood by the edge, where the trees and bushes hadn't been damaged by the fire. The two tired looking old horses seemed half asleep. They were drooping their heads in quiet resignation, their ears flicking to keep away the pestering flies....

I thought the poor things ought to have been retired ages ago! But then, if they hadn't been old, they would have been used in the German Army, and then they would most likely be dead, anyway....

During another spell of rest I was studying Margo:

It was strange to see her dishevelled like this, with hardly a trace of make-up left, and her normally wavy, black hair all limp and sweaty, sticking to her forehead!

Normally, she was quite a vain young woman, proud to have kept her trim figure after presenting Peter with two healthy little sons. I had been told that her vanity had been the cause of a good deal of worry to the other inhabitants of the household.

During those terrible first weeks after the Red Army had raged through the village, she had refused to go about in disguise like all the other women did !

She had been the only one who wouldn't wear a sack around her shoulders, leave alone rub dirt on her face to make herself look older!

All Because Of Him

"I'm not going around looking like a tramp!" She had declared; and that had been that!

But in fairness to her, it must be said that because Margo had been born in Czechoslovakia, her mother tongue was near enough to the language of the soldiers to make herself understood in Russian...and because of it, they had told her she was classed as a Non-German...so she had got away with her make-up and her pretty dresses....

"And just look at her now!" I thought, wiping my face and wishing my back would stop aching.

There was nothing to show as she went about heaving and shifting logs that she had enjoyed a pampered childhood.

Her wealthy parents had doted on her; and the nuns of the Convent, where she had been educated, had fostered her many talents. She had been taught to work with silver, wood and leather, as well as using her skill as a painter to the full.

She could design and make the most beautiful clothes: I'd seen her throw a roll of Taffeta across the floor and, with just a pin stuck here and there, cut out and sew a magnificent ball gown...all in the space of one afternoon.

And when it was finished, she painted a border of tulips all around the swirling bottom hem!

Oh, yes, Margo was clever, and she knew it! And she was very good looking, and she knew that as well!

And now she was as dirty as the rest of us, and I had to admit, working as hard as the rest of us as well! With the sun burning down on our backs, the three of us were looking forward to our break, when the farmer would take the first load home.

Every now and then some of the other teams were moving off, pushing and pulling their wobbly chariots across the uneven ground. There was a lot of grunting and groaning, as they disappeared among the trees on their way home.

I wondered how many times some of them would have to make that trip? And then, a little later, I wondered that none of them had returned for their second load so far...but I dismissed the thought.

Peter stretched to his full height once again. I could imagine his back creaking with the effort!

"Nearly time for lunch!" He said, and Margo and I straightened up as well, looking around the space that had been cleared:

Almost one and a half acres!

Around it stood the circle of surviving trees, green and beckoning with their cool shade....

I remember Margo asking:

"Don't you think it's funny that none of the other teams have come back so far?"

And I added:

"Not even the ones who live along the road to the woods and haven't got far to go!"

We all scanned the edge of the clearing for signs of returning carts, but apart from one group of people just moving off, the space was empty....

I didn't like it!

But Peter, as yet unperturbed, said that they had probably all taken an early lunch break, nothing to worry about! And he added:

"Only a few more logs, or it'll be too much for the horses. And then we'll eat."

He wiped his brow, adding yet more soot to his handsome face. His sun tan was hidden by all the dirt, and his blond hair was now a greyish yellow, clinging to his head.

We were about to pick up those last few logs, when I looked across the clearing, which lay in brilliant, glimmering sunshine.

And when I first thought I detected a slight movement under the trees on the far side, I decided it must be the contrast between light and shade... playing a trick on my vision....

Bramble thickets and a few bushy young elder trees provided a fair amount of cover over there, enough for someone who didn't want to be seen....

Surely, I must be imagining it!

But, no! There it was again:

Something like a giant green grasshopper was making its way furtively from tree to tree. And then I saw more of the same shapes, picking their way over the uneven ground, drawing closer, and, little by little, forming a circle around us.

I whispered:

"Look, Russian soldiers!"

Peter and Margo had noticed them as well by now, and with the instinct of the seasoned ex-soldier, Peter commanded:

All Because Of Him

"Quick!On the wagon!" While he shook the sleeping old farmer by the shoulder...but it was too late!

By the time the startled grandfather had clambered onto his seat, three soldiers stepped out from the thicket nearest to us and barred the way. It had been their green camouflage capes and the spiky sub machine guns which had made me think they looked like alien insects!

And alien they certainly appeared to us, with one of them now telling us in broken German:

"Old man go home... you three come! All prisoners! Go to camp!"

With that he gave the horse nearest to him a hefty whack on its hind quarters. His men jumped out of the way, and the poor frightened animal leapt forward in a mighty spurt, dragging its mate along as fast as their rickety legs could totter; and the old farmer only just managed to keep his seat....

We were left to gaze after them as they disappeared among the trees.

But not for long!

Before we had time to fully grasp what was happening, our captors persuaded us, with prods from the muzzles of their guns, to fall into line and join them on their march....

We moved off, surrounded on all sides by armed men.

Only then did we realize that we weren't the only ones caught in this latest trap: Quite a number of the men who had been leaving the clearing some time earlier were now walking with the dismal troupe....And this was the explanation why no-one had dared to return to the clearing! They had never even reached the edge of the forest on their way home, before they had been arrested!

Apparently their womenfolk had been ordered to drag their carts home as best they could.

All those women had been much older than Margo and I, who were both in our early twenties...so why had we been kept?

Images of what they might have in store for us were adding to our feelings of misery as we marched along...but we had to keep going. As soon as anyone was slacking a little, there were further prods from their guns, amid shouts of:

"Faster! Faster!" Followed by a sharp nudge forward.

I unwittingly annoyed one of the soldiers by trying to walk on the grass verge by the side of the track, because that was easier on my feet...he yelled:

For A Scrap Of Paper

"Closer! Closer!" And I felt the hard metal against my side....

Of course, the chap couldn't know that I was wearing my Uncle Fred's boots, which were miles too big, but had been the only servicable pair available....At the time I only possessed an old pair of tatty sandals, and my uncle had insisted that I wear something stronger for the thorny, splintery job with the trees!

But his boots were now chafing my feet from heel to toe, as I stumbled along on the summerdry path. There would be such blisters!

We trudged along for what seemed ages, with a few more unlucky men being added on the way, until we reached the end of the track, where it joined the cobbled country road.

One of the Russians called a halt. It was the one who had first spoken to us. He seemed to be their leader, and he now motioned us to sit in the shade of the trees by the roadside. At the same time he ordered some of his men to place themselves around us on guard.

They arranged themselves in a semi-circle between us and the road, while we flopped down on the cool grass. I thought we must look like tired old rag dolls: Unwashed and unloved, slumped any-old-how...the only difference was that rag dolls wouldn't feel afraid, even if they'd just been prodded and pushed about like our little heap of human beings!

At first, we were waiting without even talking among ourselves. I suppose we were sort of stunned.

We could see the leader and some of his cronies engaged in some sort of heated discussion. But they were sitting too far away from us, so Margo, in spite of her knowledge of Russian, couldn't get the gist of what it was all about. They seemed to be undecided about something, and we guessed it had something to do with us two females.... Their frequent glances in Margo's and my direction left no doubt in my mind that some of them wished to hang on to us as an extra bonus!

After a while, Peter urged her to ask the soldiers closest to us what it was all about.

"Go on!" He whispered. "Use your charm and get them to talk!"

But all her efforts were being met with silence. Their only response was a wide grin and a shake of the head; and after several failed attempts, Margo gave up the idea with a sigh of resignation.

The soldiers were obviously not allowed to tell us the reason for their action, so we would have to wait and see....

All Because Of Him

After a while, one of them put a hand into the pocket of his grubby tunic and fished out some gritty, fluff-covered little grey kernels: Sunflower seeds!

He smiled invitingly and offered them to us women.

Heaven knew what his pockets contained apart from the seeds, but we weren't brave enough to refuse! Most Russians I had come in contact with seemed to be fond of chewing the small kernels, and they all were experts at spitting out the minute shells....

The lot guarding us were having a sort of contest, to see who could spit furthest, inviting us to join in... and they laughed at our feeble efforts! But to our surprise, their laughter was entirely without malice!

"Dear God," I thought, like I'd done on previous encounters with members of the Red Army. "They are just boys!"

And once again, as so many times before, the whole stupid, evil futility of war and what came after made me feel heavy-hearted as well as angry.

It was all such a dreadful waste! Such a waste of time which should be spent on living, on building, instead of destroying!

A few minutes later, the men got their share of hospitality as well:

Some of the soldiers offered them a smoke!

Torn bits of paper, again fished from the depth of their pockets, were folded into a sort of pointed bag, filled with some crinkly brown weeds, and then set alight at one end....

The smell was digusting, but that didn't matter:

I believe we all felt the spell of this strange interlude, seeing friends and foes alike contentedly puffing and spitting, as if no-one had ever heard of non-fraternisation! I thought of some of the other occasions, when I had met Russians face to face, and had discovered the human being behind the alien facade.... Oh, the pity of things!

But of course, the happy state of togetherness had to end.

The leader came strutting over and planted himself in front of his captives.

The spell was broken.

We were right back to where we'd started, mixed up in an uneven cat-and-mouse game.

"Men get up!" He barked. "Lorry come...take men to camp...women go home!"

Margo's face turned pale under the grime.

In that first moment of shock, I don't believe she was helped by the relief that they seemed to have no further plans for us two. All she could think of was that she was going to lose her Peter!

And she'd only just had him back for a few weeks. He hadn't long been released from a POW-camp. So she now announced in a firm voice that she was going to stay with her husband!

Her dark eyes were flashing as if she was prepared to take on the entire Red Army!

But already the lorry could be heard rumbling towards us, and when it arrived in a cloud of dust, she was roughly pushed aside, and the captured men were jostled into the back of the vehicle. A few of the soldiers climbed in after them to act as guards, and it moved off. The rest of them marched away on foot.

The dust cloud soon swallowed the lot... and then Margo made to follow them....

I grabbed her by the arm, telling her it was futile as well as dangerous to try and keep up with a band of Russian soldiers!

But she shook off my restraining hand and said defiantly:

"I must go! I've heard them mention the name of the village where the camp is!"

It was clear by the look on her face that nothing and nobody would stop her, so I let go of her arm and said:

"Whatever you do, give a thought to your children! They don't want to lose both of you!"

But I believe at that moment, she could not think of anyone but Peter, and as she began to walk away, all she said was:

"You best get off home and tell them what's happened!"

So Margo followed the direction of the truck, while I took the road leading home. I knew her well enough: Beneath that softly feminine exterior, she was made of sterner stuff! With a good deal of luck, things might be alright....

"But I wouldn't like to be in her shoes!" I told myself, and at the same moment I realized that my own feet were now so painful, I had to take off Uncle Fred's outsize boots!

And that was the difference between Margo and me: She was stepping out briskly in her sturdy walking shoes, while I was limping all the way home on blistered bare feet!

When I got to the village, all the streets were deserted....

All Because Of Him

The windows were shuttered, and not a soul to be seen anywhere. A scary silence hung about the place. I thought that this must have been what it felt like in the days of killing and raping, looting and burning!

At last I stood outside the vicarage and rang the bell. Its jangling reverberated for a few seconds, but no-one came and opened the door....

Then there was a scurrying of feet and what sounded like a hushed discussion inside the house. I put my mouth to the key hole, like I'd done when I first arrived some weeks ago.... And after I'd shouted my name, there came the drawing of heavy bolts and the screech of the big ancient key being turned.

The door opened. I stepped into the hall.

And the whole family seemed gathered there, all staring at me in disbelief, as if I were a ghost!

Apparently the old farmer had driven the exhausted horses through the village as fast as their legs could manage.He'd shouted the story of our capture for all to hear, and he didn't stop till he arrived at my uncle's house... and when they'd opened the door, he had sobbed out his news:

"They've taken them, all of them! The Russians have got them! An' they'll all be shot!"

No wonder I had been greeted with such mixed feelings!

There had been awe, relief and disappointment, depending on who was who in the household: Only one of their number had returned.

What about the other two?

After I had finished telling them my part of the tale, we all settled down to wait in gloomy silence, dreading a knock on the door, and yet hoping and praying for it!

I remember Margo's mother sitting with her youngest grandson in her lap. She was weeping quietly. Crippled with arthritis and half blind, she must have been wondering how she could cope, if she lost both daughter and son-in-law....

Time ticked by on the old grandfather clock.

Evening came, and we still sat waiting, just waiting and listening for the sound of footsteps, the knock on the door.

I don't know whether we even had a meal during the rest of that day; I do remember someone giving me glass after glass of cool well water, when I first sat down after that gruelling walk. And someone bathed my sore feet...apart from that, everything is a blur.

For A Scrap Of Paper

At some time during the evening, some of the younger women gave the children their meal and put them to bed. And then all went quiet again.

Dusk fell.

Then came a knock on the door, followed by the shrill jangle of the bell. It shattered our numbness... and young and old started up as Margo's voice was calling to be let in!

Again the performance of bolts being drawn, the rusty noise of the big old key...and there she stood:

So weary, she almost fell into my uncle's arms!

The relief was great. But it was still marred by Peter's absense. My heart went out to my aunt and uncle: Peter was the elder of their two sons. The younger one hadn't been heard of since the days of Stalingrad....

Then Margo reported on her encounter at the soldiers' camp. She had been turned away by the guards at the entrance, but had managed to have a few words with one of them. She now knew what the raid had been in aid of...and she told us, between long drinks of water and pauses for breath:

"All they want is to find ex-soldiers who haven't been processed for proper discharge from the POW camps!"

This news was followed by sighs of relief from her audience! We knew Peter's discharge document was in order, and Margo now said:

"I know where the form is. I'll go first thing in the morning and take it to the camp. And we'll come back together!"

Brave girl; she was weary but confident, and now she got up and yawned:

"I'm tired, but I wish it were morning!"

We all followed her example. It had been a day to wear out the strongest constitution, so we went to our various quarters and fell or crawled into bed, according to each person's state of exhaustion.

Soon, everyone was asleep.

It was a peaceful night before a day of new dilemmas...but as yet, none of us could have dreamt of them!

In the morning we all had an early breakfast. Everybody was full of happy hopes, although many of us were feeling sorry for Margo, who had to make the long trek in the burning heat...quite apart from the dangers of a pretty young woman walking by herself on a road frequented mainly by soldiers.

But she didn't mind at all:

"Don't worry about me!" She laughed, "I'll be alright once I've got him out!"

And she left the room to go upstairs. She had said she'd seen the form only the other day: In one of the end drawers of the old pine wood table, which took up most of the centre of their living quarters. The drawer at the other end contained the usual assortment of cutlery and other kitchen utensils.

Now we all knew that the cramped space her family had to contend with, made it almost impossible to keep things tidy... and that it was often difficult to find a safe place for things that needed safe keeping. But added to that was the fact that Margo had a very happy-go-lucky attitude towards matters of a domestic nature! So it will be easy to understand that what followed was almost inevitable!

She seemed to be upstairs for a long time, but knowing her, I thought she was probably adding a touch of extra make-up... or something like that. But when the minutes ticked by, and she still hadn't come down, some of us began to wonder, what could be wrong? Things often got put in the wrong place; but surely that couldn't happen to such a vital piece of paper?

The thought struck me that the half blind old lady might have mislaid it?

But I dismissed the idea: She would have no cause to go to that drawer.... And so the tension rose as we listened for a sound from upstairs.

But when it came, none of us was prepared for it:

There was an infuriated scream. It was earsplitting and terrifying, and then we could hear Margo shouting and cursing in her mother tongue all the way down the stairs....

What on earth was the matter?

And in she stormed, waving a scrap of paper the size of a small envelope in the air. It was plain to see that one edge of it was rough and zig-zaggy....

She came to a stop by the side of her mother.

"What have you done with it? And where's the rest of it?" And she waved the pathetic little fragment in front of the terrified old lady's face.

The old lady knew that Margo had a terrific temper, but she obviously wasn't aware as yet what she'd done wrong! So she just stared at her angry daughter's face and said nothing.

"I've seen it only two days ago," Margo went on, "and it was in one piece then! So where's the other bit?"

By now it must have dawned on her mother what all this was about!

...“What have you done with it ? And where's the rest of it ?”...

All Because Of Him

Casting her mind back to the second day her daughter had gone to the forest, leaving her in charge of the grandchildren, she now recalled the moment when the younger boy had used his potty.

She told us, interrupted by sobs, that she had not been able to find any toilet paper... and she had remembered that Peter and Margo sometimes put bits of newspaper and other scraps into the drawer with odds and ends!

"Little-Jo was crying...so I took the first piece I came across...but I've only used half of it!"

There followed a pin-dropping silence, during which everyone's sympathy must have been divided equally between the two opponents in the dilemma. I suppose we were all wondering what Margo could possibly achieve with the remnant of that document:

It showed neither a name, nor a rank or a number, or even the place where it had been issued! And it had been printed on such poor quality paper, who could blame the old lady for thinking it was just a worthless scrap?

A little later, when Margo had got over the first shock, and her mother had stopped sobbing, my aunt asked gently:

"Do you think you can remember when, exactly, you used the paper?"

"Yesterday afternoon, just before the farmer came and told us they'd been taken away."

And then someone voiced the suggestion that we should search the box beneath the privy....

To this day, I cannot be sure whose idea it was, or whether several of us came up with it at the same time. We didn't take it seriously to start with. Maybe it was because the thought of it was too preposterous to be considered....

But the hopelessness of the situation seemed to justify even an outrageous plan such as this, even though we all knew it would be futile!

And we lost no time and set to work.

Here I must explain first about the antiquated mod-cons which were still widespread in the German countryside at the time:

Villages which were situated at the back of beyond had no proper sanitation. Better class houses had a small annexe for bodily functions; and hovels had wobbly lean-tos in the yard or at the back of the garden.

The vicarage could boast of a fairly large room in the outhouse, accessible through a side door from the main building, so the vicar needn't go out in the rain with his night shirt on, like many of his parishioners had to....

It also was fitted with a double seat: One high one and one low one, the latter with a smaller hole in the top! I used to think of it as a sort of 'Old Pompey'-contraption in the middle of the German hinterland.

In the depth below the seats was a trough-like wooden box on cast iron wheels, which would be emptied once in a while by local workmen. They would open a sort of shutter in the wall, pull out the container with long grappling hooks and drag it to the fields for manure. It was long before anyone invented the modern name of 'Recycling'!

That should suffice for a description of our amenities....

And the least said about the task confronting us, the better!

Several of us volunteered and took turns to poke about in the mess, till we couldn't stand it for another minute!

We pushed the trolley back into its place beneath the loos and went indoors, where my prudent aunt had made sure that there was a boiler full of hot water....

By the time we'd all had a wash, Margo had thought of a plan to help Peter, and she told us during lunch: We listened with mixed feelings. We had to admit that it might just work, but if it didn't, it could place her in grave danger.

She had decided to go right into the lion's den and explain her plight to the Russian Commander!

It was an idea born out of sheer desperation, but since none of us could come up with anything better, we listened quietly as she outlined her plan:

It sounded quite simple.

Margo and her mother had been able to salvage a small amount of their valuable jewellery when they fled from Czechoslovakia. They had concealed a number of gems in their clothing, including even in the baby's nappies!

They knew jewellery never loses its value, even in times when ordinary money has become worthless.... So the two women were still relatively well off, when they had arrived at the vicarage.

When Peter had come back from the POW Camp, he had praised them for the way they'd managed their escape: Babies, jewels and all!

Among that secret horde of theirs was a ring with an enormous solitaire...it belonged to Margo, and the stone was so large that my uncle had once referred to it as 'almost indecent'!

All Because Of Him

(I believe he had been goaded into making the remark after one of Margo's defiant refusals to walk about in sack cloth and ashes like all the other women...)

Anyway, she had made up her mind: The ring would have to go!

It would make an irresistible bribe. She would offer it to the pretty young woman who had told her that she was the Commandant's wife.... They'd had several friendly chats when they'd met in the village.

"She's alright." Margo declared."She seems to act as a secreta ry for the Commandant: So if anyone can get me to see him, it'll be her!"

My uncle asked:

"What exactly do you expect the Commandant to do?"

"Oh, he could write some sort of note, saying Peter is employed by him, something like that!"

This was not entirely untrue: Peter had worked at the Manor on several occasions, just like some of the other villagers.

She looked so confident, so full of eagerness to build on this faint hope....

None of us had the heart to tell her of our doubts and fears.

"Just think! If this works, I could still get him back this evening."

She left the table and went upstairs. Needless to say, she spent some time attending to her face and figure; and soon we watched her tripping along the street in her high-heeled sandals, wearing a pretty frock and, of course, she'd put on more make-up!

She might have been on her way to tea with a friend....

And as it turned out, that was more or less all it would amount to, except that the young woman was definitely not a friend!

But Margo failed to realize it to begin with....

She returned from the Manor after about an hour and gave us a glowing report about the visit:

The lady had asked her in, had given her tea, made in the big silver Samovar, and had promised to get her the note by next morning! She had said that the Commandant was not at home at present; but she would get him to see to it as soon as he returned....

Now all of us, listening to her story about the little woman and her Samovar, must have had nagging doubts about the outcome of this encounter... so Uncle Fred asked calmly:

"What about the ring?"

"Oh, she's delighted with it! It's a perfect fit!"

"But you haven't got the paper yet!" I couldn't help saying it, and I was sure it was in everybody's mind!

"That's all right," she said airily, "she told me to collect it first thing in the morning!"

My mind boggled!

That priceless diamond for what might turn out to be nothing more than an empty promise.... She must have read my thoughts.

"I'm sure she's all right, she's young and pretty, not like most of their wives, all fat like potatoes piled on top of each other!"

Some of us smiled weakly at that last remark. We couldn't see what difference it made, whether you were fat or slim, ugly or pretty: Rogues came in all shapes and sizes!

I felt sure, she had been blinded by the woman's pretence of friendliness....

However, it would have been uncharitable to labour the point, and whichever way things were to turn out next morning, it wa too late to retrieve the ring.

Once again, all the household was astir early next morning; and once again Margo proceeded up to the Manor in her best frock and shoes....

And while she was gone, we all scurried around to scrounge a few goodies to bake a cake for the homecoming: Like a kind of bribe to fate....Margo's family had been Catholics, and showing that we trusted in a good outcome might just make her Patron Saint smile on her quest!

The farmer who had lent us his wagon two days ago gave us half a dozen eggs, and the grocer let us have an advance on next week's sugar rations.

The cake turned out alright, but, as predicted, things at the Manor didn't!

In fact, you could say they'd gone disastrously wrong for poor Margo. But when we heard what had happened, we all managed to hold our tongue, and no-one said that we could have told her so!

She had arrived at the agreed time and had rang the bell, expecting to be greeted by her new friend. But it was not the pretty young woman who opened the door:

Instead she was met by a plump Russian matron, who demanded to know sternly what she wanted!

Poor Margo!

After she had stated her case,emphasizing that the Frau Commandant was expecting her, the fat lady gave her a haughty look, stuck out her bosom, and said:

"I am Frau Commandant!" When she saw how the visitor was taken aback by her assertion, she added:

"I - REAL wife! Other one just his WOMAN!"

After Margo had recovered enough to state her case in full, the real Frau Commandant had weighed up the situation; and she lost no time in taking advantage of the young person's predicament.

Looking her up and down, she saw the watch on Margo's wrist....

The watch was not as precious as the ring had been, but it was costlier than any treasure the lady had ever come across in her own spartan country. It was pure gold inlaid with small diamonds, and Madam decided it would do very well!

She took Margo by the arm and steered her into the entrance hall.... She said she would ask her husband to write the necessary document, adding:

"You give me watch. I show husband!"

But this time, the guest was in no mood to yield the prize. She said firmly:

"You give me paper - I give you watch!"

The woman must have seen the determination in Margo's face, and so she had disappeared into the inner sanctum of the Manor, from where she emerged in due course with a piece of paper all stamped and signed....

After Margo had parted with the watch, she brought the note for us all to inspect and admire. Then she went to their room, changed into her walking shoes and set out for the camp.

And all the time she was gone, the ones left behind were praying fervently that things wouldn't go wrong THIS time!

Because we knew what it said on the piece of paper she had in her pocket: The Commandant had written that Peter was needed at the Manor to carry out some repairs....

Would the ones in charge of the camp be willing to let him go for that reason?

Again a day of waiting and hoping. And then, at last, by late afternoon there came a knock on the door:

And there they stood, hand in hand like newly-weds!

We were weak at the knees with relief, and then the aunt brewed a huge pot of 'Ersatz-Kaffee',(made from barley, I think), and we ate the cake....

After we'd feasted our eyes on the happy couple,and our insides with food and drink, Uncle Fred asked how the guards had reacted to the phoney certificate?

Peter looked at his brave young wife and told us that most of them hadn't been in a position to react to anything, because they'd been blind drunk, having just had one of their extensive boozing sessions! And Margo added:

"Anyway, the one I showed the paper to couldn't read! He was holding it upside down. So I just pointed to Peter and said, that he was the one they must let go! - And that was that!"

Point Of No Return

End of August,1945. Nothing moved in the sleepy village. Not a farm dog or cat was astir. The silence of the warm August night embraced even the headquarters of the local Russian Commander in the Manor House.

Normally there was a great deal of noise and commotion in that place, until well into the small hours....

Russian soldiers love their Vodka, and the reason for the frequent revelries was usually a binge by its occupants!

So when the Manor lay quietly among the circle of ancient beech trees, it usually meant that they were having a boozing party, or an orgy or both in some other garrison.

In the old vicarage, too, the lights had gone out.

The aged parson and his wife had retired to bed hours ago; and the many refugees from various parts of Europe all lay in peaceful oblivion.

The vicarage, with its many large and small rooms, was full to the roof tops in the literal sense! Most of the people who were now living in it were related in some way or other: There was the son of the vicar, recently discharged from a POW Camp, and with him were his wife and two small sons, as well as his mother-in-law.

There were daughters of the old couple with their children; and there were my own parents and I, all squeezed in somewhere.

From the ground floor to the cob-webby corners of the attic, there wasn't a niche that wasn't occupied by someone with nowhere else to go.

I had been given a small room beneath the pigeon loft and lay listening to the faint night-noises. All seemed quiet outside, but from the tiny box room next to me I could hear my father's gentle snores through the flimsy partition.

He had arrived a few days ago in search of my mother. who had been staying with her sister, the vicar's wife. My father had taken her there, after their flat in Hanover was lost in one of the town's last air-raids; and they were now preparing for the trip back to Hanover....

I was happy for them to be together again.

It was the thought of their journey to the West which was keeping me awake: I didn't feel at all happy about it, because it was becoming a difficult, in certain areas even a dangerous undertaking, to attempt leaving the Russian Sector.

The Soviets were well aware that most people didn't like to live in the part of Germany over which they ruled: People said it was worse than before....But the Russian Authorities were determined to stop the drain to the West.

I had been discussing the many obstacles of the trip with both parents until late that evening, and Father had asked:

"Why don't you come with us?"

"I can't, I must be near Magdeburg, in case Karl comes back!"

"You'll be much safer in Hanover!"

I knew this to be true, but I also knew that if my marriage was to survive at all, I must be near the people Karl would always put first: His parents....

So I had said wretchedly:

"I know; but I've got to stop here."

Father had given me a long, searching look and asked:

"Don't you think he would find you wherever you are, if he really loves you?"

And now there was a stab of pain deep inside me, because of that little word 'IF'!

Karl had been my first love, and all had seemed well with our marriage to begin with. But his parents disapproved of me, showing it plainly in word and action.

They and I seemed to exist on different planes.

And they were constantly nagging about my love for painting, writing, reading and 'all that rubbish', as his mother referred to it....

During my last visit to them, I had been waiting for a pass to cross the river Elbe. And her words at the end of the last big scene were still haunting me!

I had wanted to see how my mother and the others in the small village across the Elbe had fared since the end of the war; and mother-in-law had said I was going 'gallivanting'. She had called my search a 'Wild goose chase'!

I'd had no news, didn't know whether the village had survived the first onslaught of the victorious Russian Army!

It certainly hadn't been a question of going gallivanting. I simply had to find out what had happened to them!

And during that argument his mother had left me in no doubt:

There would be no room for me in their midst, unless I adapted to their way of life...she had stated quite plainly:

"My boy has promised me - if his wife doesn't fit in with us, she'll have to go!"

There was no answer to that.

I didn't want to argue with her! I was terrified of losing him whatever I said! So I had left them, as soon as I got my pass to cross the river, and had gone on with my quest to see what was happening at my uncle's vicarage!

Now, lying on my hard, narrow iron bedstead in that little attic room, I thought:

"Maybe Dad is right: Going back to Hanover would be a testing point... I'd know whether Karl *really* cares."

It was no good worrying about it all night,though! And I turned over and went to sleep, but not for long:

A slight fluttering in the pigeon loft above woke me, and I wondered what could have disturbed the birds? They appeared to settle for a moment, and then the fluttering began again....And this time I could hear a rumbling noise and some raised voices.They seemed to come from the crossroads just beyond the church....

It was the sound of a lorry.

"Nothing unusual in that," I thought, "just the soldiers, coming home from their party. The birds caught the sound sooner than I did."

But then there was more rumbling, coming from another direction this time - another lorry? The engine noises stopped....Instead there was a great deal of shouting and yelling.

"Maybe two vehicles have met in that tight place near the crossroads," I thought, "and they're arguing who's to give way!"

The streets were narrow and winding. It would be very difficult for two lorries to get past each other, especially if they were navigated by drunken drivers!

After a few minutes, the voices of the two parties were taking on a more aggressive note. It was definitely not a friendly encounter out there beyond the church....

By now I could hear someone moving about in the large room at the opposite end of the attic, where my cousin Peter and his family were housed.

I got out of bed and put on my old mac, which had to serve as a dressing gown for want of the real thing. I went and opened my bedroom door: And there stood Margo, Peter's wife. Her black hair was disshevelled, but she was quite calm.

She said:

"Peter wants us all to get up! There may be trouble, they're drunk!"

"Oh they're *always* drunk at this time of night!" I protested.

But Margo had been brought up in Czechoslovakia. She knew enough of the Russian language to get the drift of any conversation, heated or otherwise....And she now insisted:

"There are two lorries, and neither of the drivers wants to give way. I heard them arguing!"

"I still can't see why we should be in danger because of that!"

"Because they're spoiling for a fight! And afterwards they'll be looking for scapegoats - among the villagers!"

"Oh, what about my father? He hasn't got a pass!"

"Peter says, he and your father might have to go into hiding, if things go wrong out there! But we'll wait and see!"

And she went back to her family.

However, she left the doors open between my room and theirs, so we could call across to each other....

So now I had to tell my parents, whose tiny cubby-hole of a room was accessible only through mine. I felt sick at heart:

Why should something like this threaten their peace of mind, when they were just trying to sum up courage to set out for home!

But they had heard us, and now they were both standing in the low doorway, asking me what they should do.

"Nothing for the moment, just get dressed quickly and then we'll just wait and listen."

And as if my words had been a cue, we heard the sound of engines being restarted.... Some more shouting of what was surely Russian expletives! And then the roar as they began to move....

They were going!

We all breathed a sigh of relief - and at the same moment we heard a shot!

No-one knew who had fired it, or whether it had been aimed at anyone. It might have been fired in anger or out of sheer bravado and exhuberance:

But it echoed around the village like a whole volley of shots, and it was the signal for all hell to break loose!

We figured that the soldiers in both lorries thought they were being attacked: And as was usual, when they were intoxicated, they didn't wait to find out who the attacker was....They just started firing wildly to right and left, while the drivers careered through the streets in opposite directions....

After a few minutes, the lorry from the other garrison must have arrived at the point where the driver should have turned off in the first place:

It rumbled out of the village, and the shooting stopped.

We could hear our local Russian crew shouting and jeering as they were turning into the drive to the Manor. Then all was quiet, but for how long?

The inhabitants of the groundfloor seemed to be up and about as well now. Some of the children were crying.

I went downstairs to ask my Uncle Fred, what we should do; and I found both him and my aunt in the process of calming down the young women and their infants and toddlers.

They were a courageous pair, my uncle and aunt: He was in his mid-seventies, and she was about sixty-four or five at the time! And they seemed to have the situation well in hand: The children were probably crying because their sleep had been interrupted, rather than from fear.

The ones who were afraid were the adults; because there was by now little doubt that a raid on all the houses in the village was imminent!

Uncle Fred took my arm and led me away from the others. When we'd got to the bottom of the stairs, he said:

"Your father's got to get out of the house!"

"But how?"

"Ask Peter, and be quick!" And as he turned to go back to the others, he smiled his kind, reassuring smile and added:

"When they come here, I'll delay them as long as possible!"

I pictured the front door of the ancient house: It was bolted and barred, with all the screws deeply imbedded into thick oak; but how long could it withstand guns and rifle butts?

When I got upstairs, I found Peter bent over a pile of bedlinen. He was tying some sheets together....

It seemed a silly question to ask him what he was doing, since it was obvious, that he was making a rope!

But it was such a crazy situation to be in, my mind refused to believe what was going on!

Peter said, without looking up:

"You can see what I'm doing. go and make one for your father! We got to get out of the windows!"

I knew it made sense, but I still stared at him, sort of trying to take in what it meant, and he went on:

"Your father'll have to get onto the summer house roof below your window, and I'll get onto the washhouse on our side!"

I protested:

"But Dad'll never manage that! The window is too small! And on a ROPE!"

Peter was deadly serious, though:

"It's the only way. No-one can spot us there from the street because of the high walls, and on the garden side we're covered by trees and bushes."

When I still stood there, he said sharply:

"Get a move on! And don't open the windows or the outside shutters until your lights are out!"

When I told my parents, they took it without demur; and Mother began to strip the beds with shaking hands, while Father got into some warmer clothes. Then I set about tying the unwieldy sheets into knots, hoping they wouldn't come undone!

My heart was heavy thinking of the older people under this roof. They had lived through two world wars, and yet there was still no peace for them!

When the knots seemed tight enough, Mother and I secured the rope to the foot of my bed... and I felt as if I was moving in a bad dream, from which I would awake any moment....

141

All Because Of Him

But it was all too real: As the lights in Peter's room went out, we switched off ours as well. I thought how easy it would be for Peter's lithe young body to get out and onto the roof below! I still couldn't imagine how my father was going to squeeze through the tiny opening of my window!

"Poor Dad!" I thought, feeling choked as he patted my cheek reassuringly, and I only just managed to blink back the tears...no time for that now!

I drew back the curtains, and he opened the window.

It had two wings, which were locked with a swivel to a centre bar; and the bar also held the hooks in place which secured the outside shutters by night.

He leaned out to gauge the drop to the roof. It was only just visible, because there was no moon that night.

Suddenly, the night became filled with shouts and harshly barked commands, and the orders had hardly been given, when all the front doors of the neighbourhood seemed to receive a simultaneous battering from the soldiers' rifles.

The din was terrifying!

Then I felt a sudden inrush of air, which ceased again almost immediately:

Peter must have got out safely, and Margo had lost no time, had closed the window and made everything look normal....

Whereas we were struggling to get my father across the window sill! Both Mother and I begging him to hurry!

Oh , his legs were so long and rather stiff and the opening so small.... The days when he loved dancing or take me ice-skating were long in the past; and in recent years, he'd often had trouble breathing.

But Mother and I cajoled him and pushed him, and implored him not to let go of the rope too soon, once he was outside:

"You mustn't land with a thud!" We told him.

I don't remember how we finally squeezed him through....

And while he was stiffly letting himself down the rope, I found myself lapsing into that state of extreme tension, when some trivial detail can catch the eye and make one want to laugh:

And so, in the middle of our struggle, with the clamour of the mob in the street growing more insistent every minute, I suddenly had to think of an illustration from 'Alice In Wonderland':

Father reminded me of the picture where the Dormouse is being stuffed into the teapot! The thouht was followed at once by a feeling of guilt; but looking back, the comparison was perhaps not all that far fetched.

My hands were holding on to the upper end of the rope, and as soon as he had landed, I started to pull it in for all I was worth!

While I was untying it from the leg of the bed, knowing that we would have to hide it somewhere, I could hear increased banging and battering against the door downstairs:

Dear Uncle Fred! He was still holding out! I was sure he'd bought us enough time!

At last I held the pile of knotted sheets in my arms. There was no time to separate them, They'd have to be hidden in one piece.

Behind the wardrobe might be best!

I was heaving against the heavy piece of old mahogany to widen the gap just a fraction, when I heard a shot somewhere below!

It echoed upwards from the hall, and now the shouting and yelling was within our walls!

I heard Margo race downstairs and guessed what she was trying to do:

She was hoping to use her knowledge of the soldiers' language to act as go-between! Maybe she even thought she could prevent the mob from coming upstairs.

If only she could stall them for just a minute or two!

Could Mother give me a hand with the wardrobe? But she was slumped in a chair, locked in by her fear...I didn't think she even noticed what I was doing. I'd have to stash the thing out of sight as best I could: I pushed and pushed...it was an awful lot of linen for such a narrow space!

The rumpus downstairs was going on unabated, and now I could hear Margo's voice at the bottom of the stairs. She kept saying:

"NO MEN HERE! Go home! No men in this house - only old grandfather downstairs! GO HOME!"

But their trampling footsteps were making their way upstairs without pausing, and when they had reached the attic landing, they divided into two groups.

One lot went with Margo, and the others burst into my room, only a split second after I'd pushed the last awkward corner of sheet out of sight! I straightened up, thinking that we'd managed safely, and they wouldn't find anything....

There were four of them. They kept shouting:

All Because Of Him

..."We find men here—you be shot"...

"Where men? We find men here, you all be shot!"

And they proceeded to give the place a thorough going-over.

Mother still hadn't moved, but I saw that her lips were forming half audible words of prayer....

The soldiers were by now not only drunk from their Vodka. The excitement of the manhunt seemed to have added to the effect of the alcohol!

They had begun their search by poking their rifles into every cavity which might conceal a human form. After that they pulled apart the bedding and tore the clothes out of the wardrobe. Then they scraped the long muzzles of the rifles along the floor under the beds, all the time shouting their battle-cry of:

"We find men - you be shot!"

Only three of them were doing the actual searching, and the one who did not take part was probably the most dangerous of them all:

He was standing in the doorway, with his hands in his pockets; his eyes watching every movement of us, as well as of his men.

I was sure he wouldn't miss a thing!

It suddenly struck me that his cap, which was perched jauntily to one side of his head, was green: the colour of the Secret Police!

Dear God, that was all we needed!

I wondered if he'd noticed that there had been no sheets on the beds, even before they had started the search?

But no, most of them had never even slept in a conventional bed, leave alone between the cool comfort of clean linen! And even if he HAD noticed it, there was nothing I could do about it now.

After a few minutes, one of the searchers stopped his prodding of inanimate objects and turned his attention to me instead.

He took out his revolver, poked it against my ribs and said:

"You tell us where men are! Or you all be shot!"

It was beginning to sound like a record with its needle stuck!

And suddenly, the icy calm, which had come to my aid so often before, asserted itself: Even though I was terrified, I now smiled at him innocently and said in my friendliest voice:

"Can't you see? No men here; only old Mamushka and myself! And take away that gun, it hurts!"

But he kept it there, pressed tightly against my chest. It was very uncomfortable, because there was only the old mac and a thin nightdress between my skin and the hard steel.

He then decided to change tactics and tried a different approach. With his free hand he pointed to my mother and said coaxingly:

"We only want men! You tell us... then Mamushka and you be alright!"

I was still cool on the outside, repeating over and over again that there was no man here. But it was very difficut to remain calm as the minutes ticked by, especially when I looked at my mother, who seemed to have shrunk within the last half hour. She appeared barely able to support herself on the chair. Tears were streaming down her cheeks. She had ceased praying.

Trying for the umpteenth time to make the soldier understand that there was no-one hidden in the place, I pointed from the wardrobe and its contents, which were strewn around the floor, to the empty beds in both rooms.

Until now I had been playing my part correctly, but until now, I had been facing the door and the soldiers....

Then I half turned, with the gun still tightly pressed against me; and while I was looking for some more evidence to show that we really weren't hiding anyone in these two small rooms, I saw the vital detail that I had overlooked!

The detail that could undo us all:

In the desperate hurry to hide the sheets I hadn't had time to close the window before the men burst in....

Now window and shutters were wide open, and the curtains were swaying in the night air!

My knees wanted to give way: Surely of all the things which could have gone wrong, this must be the worst! Yet until that moment I hadn't even given it a thought!

I prayed:

"Please, God, don't let me start shivering!"

Oh, how I prayed! I knew that the gun would transmit my shaking fear to the hand holding it. I even asked God to make something happen, so that none of our befuddled assailants would draw the right conclusion from that dark open space....

It is easy to say later that what happened was coincidence, but then, what is coincidence?

While I was trying to steady myself with a few deep breaths, there was a sudden inrush of wind.... Someone must have opened a door downstairs, and now the curtains were billowing wildly into the room....

The soldier withdrew his gun and walked over to the window.

"Now," I thought, "any second now! He'll lean out and discover the figure on the roof!"

I wished he'd pulled the trigger on me before it had come to this! Then I shouldn't have to face what would happen next! They would take my father away, and we should never see him again, because I had failed....

The tension bore down on me like a physical weight. While the man took the few steps towards the window, time seemed to stand still. It really was like watching a film in slow motion.

I couldn't move. My heart was pounding right up into my head.

But what happened then, was hard to believe... and at the time it seemed like a miracle:

Maybe the soldier, flushed with excitement, with beads of sweat trickling into his tight-fitting collar, was feeling irritated by the cold draught streaming in... or perhaps he thought that we might try to escape into the blackness out there....

Whatever it was, no-one could tell what made him act as he did:

He paused by the window.

I saw him place one hand on the sill - but he did not put out his head to discover what the night held hidden....

No, he slowly tucked the gun into his belt...then he sort of flexed his shoulders, stretched out his arms and gripped both halves of the window! He drew them close and fixed the swivel....

Then he turned to me, grinning all over his sweaty face. He seemed pleased with himself, as if he were saying:

"There! I've put a stop to that!"

I didn't dare look at my mother.

The one with the green cap would notice if we so much as batted an eyelid, or breathed a sigh of relief!

"You right, no man here!" The soldier said now. "But we come back! We keep looking!"

He drew out his gun again, waved it towards his comrades and motioned them to leave. They trooped out of the room towards the stairs, where they met the others, who had been equally unsuccessful in Peter's quarters.

They left the vicarage.

All Because Of Him

But we knew from past experience that the search wouldn't be called off for days. So what were we going to do with our two men on the roof?

I went across to Margo, who had a couple of blankets ready to drop down to them. It might be hours before they could leave their hiding place.

"When it's gone quiet, we'll put up a ladder for your father. I dare say Peter'll jump down without help."

As the blanket sailed down towards Peter, Margo asked him in a whisper:

"What next?"

His voice was barely louder than the stirring of leaves:

"Go next door; tell the farmer we need to use the loft in his barn. He's got a place behind the hay for this kind of thing!"

"Right! I won't be long!"

Once more Peter's voice came back:

"Take the back lane, and don't get caught!"

She pulled her head back, closed shutters, window and curtains and handed me a blanket for my father. I left her as she was searching among the pile of clothes strewn around the floor. She told me that she was looking for her black evening cape.

I guessed why: She would be no more than a shadow, gliding past the bushes in the alleyway leading to the farm....

I went across to my room. Mother was still sitting motionless in her chair. I dropped the blanket down to my father and told him that we'd help him down as soon as it seemed safe.

And now I, too, closed shutters, window and curtains, and then I led Mother to Peter's room, where Margo's mother was waiting quietly, with her youngest grandson held on her lap. I took the whole little troupe downstairs, where we could all be together, and where we could discuss what had to be done.

As we entered the kitchen, where all the household seemed to be assembled, I heard the back door softly open and close: Margo was on her way....

I had to admire her. She had not once given way to her emotions, whereas I was feeling decidedly shaky by now. I wanted nothing more than a place to flop down on, somewhere to wait for the shivering to pass.

Someone was pulling some chairs towards the warm kitchen stove for the newcomers, and one of my younger cousins was ladling out some hot soup...(tomorrow's ration, I suspected!).

Everybody seemed to be there. It was an almost peaceful scene, all of them sipping the near-scalding liquid with a sort of animal satisfaction, content to sit quietly after the ordeal....

Suddenly, I remembered the shot we'd heard, when the soldiers came in! So far, I hadn't had a chance to find out what had happened on the groundfloor. Had anyone been hurt?

I looked around the room....

Then I noticed my Uncle Fred. He was sitting stiffly in his old Carver chair, while his wife was fitting a sling round his right arm and shoulder. I rushed over to them and asked:

"Has he been hit?"

"Yes," said my aunt, "but not by the shot you heard. They fired that to force the lock. It was when they burst in: One of them hit him across the shoulder with his rifle butt. I think his collar bone is broken."

"How barbaric!" I thought, "to do that to an old man!"

Then it struck me that, until that moment, I had never thought of my Uncle Fred as old. He had always been my favourite uncle, with a lovely smile which used to crinkle right up to his eyes....

But now, for the first time, I saw how age had caught up with him: He looked worn and tired.

Someone handed me a cup of soup, and while I was sipping it, the kitchen door opened, and Margo came in.

She slid out of her cape, and together with the garment she now seemed to discard the composure she had shown up to now. She sank into the nearest chair, panting for breath, and she even declined the soup someone held out to her. She shook her head, her lovely black hair hanging down over her face, and after a minute or so she said:

"Just let me get my breath back! I've been running like a hare with the hounds after him!"

"Did you get to the farmer?" I asked.

"Oh,yes! Everything's ready for them. But we'd better hurry! I overheard some soldiers: They'll start searching again as soon as it gets light."

I wondered, how on earth she had managed to squeeze past any soldiers in that narrow little back-lane!

So I asked:

"Were they in the LANE?"

"No," she said with a conspiratorial grin, "I crept past the Manor on my way back!"

I stared at her. She was supposed to have taken the lane both ways - trust her to be such a daredevil!

"Don't say anything, please!" She whispered. "At least now we know what's up!"

"Do you think it's safe to get my father down yet? It won't be dark for much longer!"

Before she could answer, a voice from the kitchen door said:

"I'll get him down. You two get some warm clothes and a couple more blankets!"

It was Peter. He had jumped from the roof, as Margo had expected. Now he turned to his mother and asked:

"Can you pack some food for a few days? After that, someone will have to bring us more on a pretext... Father could drop in on a casual visit, or mother pop in for a chat?"

And now my aunt really came into her own!

She started bustling about between kitchen and larder, cutting and scraping.... And before we knew it, she had assembled a pile of sandwiches, which could deceive anyone into thinking there was no food shortage!

By the time Margo and I returned to the kitchen with bundles of blankets and warm clothes, there was a haversack filled with flasks of milk and coffee as well as the prepared food.

The men were ready.

We opened the back door, and my father and Peter crept out into the night, like a pair of burglars carrying their haul....

It was still dark, but the stars were waning. In the East the first glimmer of daylight was painting the sky a lighter shade of blue.

We heard he faint crunching of their shoes, as they made their way through the quiet garden and out into the lane. Then the silence swallowed them up. And only a few seconds later, the first cockerel sounded his morning cry. We closed and bolted the back door, knowing that they'd be only just in time.

Back in the kitchen, no-one spoke for a while. It was as if everyone's thoughts were out there in the barn: Imagining how the farmer would guide them up the steep ladder into the far corner of the hay-filled loft. The hideout had been prepared a long time ago, soon after the first raids had taken place....

Point Of No Return

Once up there, they would be left in the pitch-dark; and after the farmer had built a wall of hay across the tiny nook, he would climb down and take the ladder with him. It would be placed somewhere in the orchard, so that no suspicion would fall on the barn.

After that, the two of them would be in their corner for good or ill. No-one knew for how long....

No-one saw them for days on end. They were well hidden.

The vicarage seemed oddly quiet. The only people leaving it once in a while were my uncle and aunt....

Who would have suspected that the old gentleman was carrying packed lunches tucked into the triangular bandage, which was supporting his injured collar bone?

And why shouldn't the vicar's wife, on her way to place fresh flowers on the altar, call on the farmer's wife for a chat?

In the basket she was carrying, beneath some late roses, bunches of ivy and a few hollyhocks, there were several items which certainly weren't meant for the altar....

But then, no-one must know that there were things like clean socks, wrapped around the odd bottle of home-made wine, hidden beneath the greenery for the church.

My aunt told us how the farmer's wife then completed the next stage of the deliveries: On certain days, she altered her normal routine slightly, collecting the eggs from the barn first, leaving the orchard and the henhouse till last....

She also seemed to have developed a preference for collecting the eggs in a deep pail, instead of a shallow basket! And the pail always had bits of sacking across the top!

It was most odd!

But, in all the days the men were hidden there, no-one seemed to notice.

Peter and Father had to keep very quiet in their den, had to be constantly on the alert for any noises from below, or from somewhere outside.... Only at a given signal would Peter remove one of the floor boards and lower a basket, such as were used for bringing logs indoors.

The woman would transfer the goods to it, often adding a little extra from her own pantry...and once the basket had been hoisted aloft again, the board was replaced, and she carried on with her egg round.

For our two hideaways life in the confined space must have been far from comfortable, quite apart from the need for strict silence: In the cramped conditions, they were almost roasted by the heat of the August sun, burning down on the corrugated roof all day.

And in contrast, the nights were very chilly indeed, because of the way the walls of the barn were constructed: In order to let the hay breathe, there were holes alternating with the bricks along the entire wall!

It was good for the hay, but cold comfort for the humans!

After five more days the Russians called off their search. They hadn't been near the vicarage or the farm since that fearful night. For some reason they had concentrated on the surrounding fields and woods, where they had caught a few unfortunate farm workers from a neighbouring village.

After that, all went quiet.

We waited for another day, just to be sure all was well, and then, late one evening, the farmer carried the ladder back into the barn and brought our two men down to earth.

When they arrived at the vicarage, they looked like tramps!

All that time without shaving or a wash! They had slept in their clothes every night for fear of a surprise attack, and when Margo rushed up to give Peter a joyous hug, he waved an imaginary bell at her, calling out:

"Unclean! Unclean!"

It was true: We could smell them as soon as they came into the kitchen! And again it was my aunt who rose magnificently to the occasion. As soon as she'd been sure that we could expect them home, she had lit the fire under the big copper boiler in the washhouse, and now everything was ready. We led the smelly wanderers to the steaming outhouse, where my mother and Margo had laid out clean clothes, piles of towels and bars of carbolic soap.

And then we left the two men to be scrubbed from head to toe by their spouses.

Meanwhile the other adult members of the household were assembling in the dining room, where the aunt had laid the table for a 'Coming-home-feast'....

Surely her store room must have had unsuspected reserves: It had yielded up ingredients for one of her famous plum cakes!

Eventually the two couples emerged from their ordeal of scrubbing and scraping, and the men looked like their old familiar selves again, ready to sit down and eat with the rest of us.

So we ate all the cake....

And long after we'd finished, and the table had been cleared, we still sat talking over the events of the past week.

At last my father looked around from one happy face to the other. He cleared his throat and said:

"Well, thank God, that's all over now! And thank you all for taking such risks! But I think it's time we started our trip home as soon as we can now!"

He looked at my mother and took her hand, adding:

"Tomorrow we'll have a rest, but we'll leave the day after."

Peter grinned at him and said:

"Yes, you better go before another drunken driver decides he's come to a point of no return and starts a rampage!"

I believe we all felt the same:

Go while the going is good!

Now my father's eyes met mine across the table. There was a question in them....I smiled at him and nodded. I had made up my mind to go with them and make a fresh start.

Then it would be up to Karl when he returned... IF he was still alive....

And if it were true what his mother had said, I would have to face it. Every night for the past week, I had turned her ominous words over and over in my mind, when she had said I would have to go if I didn't fit in.

Try as I might,I still couldn't imagine what she had meant by one of her parting shots, on the day I had started out for my trek across the river. It had puzzled me ever since:

She had said with a smirk that she would soon make Karl realize how I had been carrying on while he was away!

Carrying on what, and with whom?

I knew she was a liar.

But by now I also knew my husband's weakness as far as his parents were concerned! What weapon did she have to beat me in this battle? I hadn't done anything wrong!

Then I thought, still hoping against hope, that, after all, Karl had married *me*! Not his mother! And I still could not imagine life without him....

So I had decided to put it to the test!

And now Father reached across the table and held my hand for a minute: He knew it hadn't been an easy decision. But nothing more needed to be said between us.

All Because Of Him

The following day, Mother and I started sorting the few things we were going to pack, while Father was walking up and down in the garden outside, exercising his muscles. They were still stiff from the days in confinement. We could see him stretching his arms above his head and squaring his shoulders, as he paced to and fro between the low box wood hedges. Once in a while he would walk right around the far side of the darkly shining pond, making his way back past the big old chestnut tree, where in the past all the family used to gather on fine afternoons....

We had spent many happy hours sitting in the cool shade, having meals outdoors, reading, talking...before the darkness came....

I wondered if he was thinking of those happier times?

Mother and I were packing only a few clothes and the food needed for the journey; no more than would fit into two rucksacks and her small holdall. It was necessary to travel light, to be ready to drop everything and run, if need be.

My mother had recovered her composure after the night of the raid; but the new ordeal lying ahead was making her tense in spite of my efforts to cheer her up.

I kept telling her that Dad had come through the forbidden area on his way here without any trouble, so why shouldn't we be alright on the way back?

But I knew only too well that this wouldn't allay her fears:

Everybody was aware of the risks connected with an attempt to leave the Russian Sector. If we were caught, it might at best mean a night in the cellars of the Russian Guards. But if the captors felt inclined to be severe, it could mean transportation to one of their camps, no-one knew where....

So she had every reason to feel uneasy.

"I couldn't bear another separation from your father!"

I tried to put as much conviction as possible into my voice:

"Just think, it will be like the old days! If the weather is fine, we'll pretend we're on a long hike!"

"That's silly talk!" She said, a defensive sharpness creeping into her voice, " the old days are gone!"

It had been thoughtless of me to mention those days:

It was bound to remind her of the loss of my younger sister not very long ago!

So we said nothing for a while, and she just sighed sadly and went on sorting the things to take and things to leave behind....

I remember how all through that last day, people seemed to engage only in small talk. The tension was affecting all but the children.

It was a relief to retire to bed early. We were going to catch the first train, and everybody wanted to come along to say Goodbye.

As I settled down on my iron bedstead, I thought:

"Tomorrow! Tomorrow I'm going home! Oh, roll on tomorrow!"

And then I slept.

And tomorrow dawned and turned into today, and it was a lovely day for walking!

First there would be the two mile stretch to the little branch line station, then a short train ride to Magdeburg.

From there, another branch line train would take us to the border of the No-go-area, where everything came to a dead end.

After that would come the tricky part of crossing the dangerous zone, uninhabited and full of menace....

But once through that, we would arrive somewhere in the region of Helmstedt, the first small town in the West.

There, we would leave the fear behind us!

Oh, how I was looking forward to that moment!

During breakfast on that last morning, I felt almost guilty:

I looked at the familiar faces of all the people sitting around the table, knowing they were being left behind....

We had been together in many a tight spot, and I wished I could have taken them with me to a place where there was no Manor House full of drunken soldiers, no raids on innocent villagers and no deportation to places no-one ever came back from....

But even those thoughts could by now only touch on the fringe of my happiness at leaving.

I even found myself hoping that Karl might turn up in Hanover one day, in spite of his mother's prophetic threats!

Perhaps he would decide to stay in the West with me!

While I had been tying the strings of our rucksacks earlier on, after packing the food parcels the aunt had got ready for us, my father had said:

"You know, if Karl comes to find you, I could quite easily arrange for him to get a job in the office."

And I had joined into making plans along those lines....

All Because Of Him

Oh, such plans, and such dreams!

We would be able to start a new life. It would be like the times before we lost our home, and before he had to leave for the last days of the fighting....

And then we were all walking towards the station, and all the ablebodied inhabitants of the vicarage were accompanying us to wave their Farewells. It was like a big family outing on a bright and promising morning.

After a while, I found myself at the back of the throng, walking beside my favourite cousin.

"When times are better, you must come and visit us," I told her, and she said, laughing:

"Only if I don't have to go through the middle bit!"

It was all quite light-hearted, like people chat, when there is not much time left, and everything else has been said.

We were following the others at a slightly slower pace, when I suddenly felt a prickly sensation at the back of my neck....

I'd heard it said, that this can happen when one senses the presence of someone approaching from behind,(maybe a sort of animal instinct, a remnant from our distant past?).

Whatever it was, I felt compelled to turn and see who was following us!

I stopped and looked back along the road. The sun was in my eyes, so at first I could only make out the distant figure of someone pushing a bike.

When the figure came closer, I saw it was a man. Soon, he was near enough to make out his features....

I rubbed my eyes, and I looked again: It was no mirage! He was thinner then when I had last seen him, and his hair was very short, POW-style....

But it was Karl!

Forgotten were my fears for our happiness! Abandoned in one glorious moment were all my great plans for going home:

He was alive! He was here! Nothing else mattered!

I rushed up to him, wanting to hold him, to weep at his neck with sheer joy and relief....

But as my arms went around his shoulders, I felt him stiffen, as if he recoiled from my touch....

A stab of fear went through me.

But immediately, my heart found an excuse, in an attempt not to face the truth:

"He is holding his bike," my heart said, "so he can't hug me!"

156

Point Of No Return

But the voice of fear flashed back:

"Why doesn't he drop the ruddy bike? It's six months since he's last seen you!"

The heart again tried to fan the small spark of hope that was left:

"Maybe it's because of what he's been through as a prisoner?"

But by now, fear was growing into certainty:

He had gone home to his parents first!

It wouldn't have taken his mother long to put the poison in...even though I still didn't know what she could have said to spoil things.

But everything WAS spoilt. I could feel it, see it in his eyes, they seemed to be accusing me of something... If only I knew what it was! Only one thing was clear: His mother had won the battle. My arms sank away from him limply. They seemed like a dead weight, like I felt inside by now!

So far, only the cousin, who had been walking by my side, had seen what was happening. She now stood watching silently, perhaps wondering at that strange re-union....

I remember thinking:

"I mustn't let my parents see how I feel. It would be an extra burden, now that they'll have to go without me!"

And so I called out to them:

"Look, who's here!"

They all turned around, their faces reflecting their different reactions: There was disbelief, followed by surprise, and then pleasure on most of them. Perhaps they all thought how lucky I was!

My mother couldn't seem to take it in. She was staring at Karl with a sort of stonily bewildered look.

And then I met my father's eyes....

Oh, his dear face!

It had clouded over with such sadness, such disappointment!

And it wasn't just the thought of having to make the trip without me....No. It was much more than that:

He knew that now I had reached my 'Point-of-no-return'.

157

Buttered Rolls and Belly Pork

January 1947. A bitterly cold day. I stood in front of the imposing old building which had once been a boys' Grammar school. It had been taken over by the Red Army soon after the war, and its halls were now echoing to the voices of Russian children whose parents were stationed in Magdeburg.

I was trying to sum up courage to enter the place, because, from this morning onwards, I was to work there as a charwoman. Looking up at the high granite walls with dozens and dozens of many-paned windows, I told myself:

"At least I'll be indoors in this freezing weather!"

It would certainly be better than the only alternative I had been offered at the Employment Exchange: Carting rubble on the bomb sites of the ravaged city! A man with a dead-pan face had looked at me coldly from across his counter and declared:

"Unless you accept one of these jobs, we shall withhold your next ration card."

He had pushed back my note from the surgeon, which stated that I must not do any heavy lifting for the next six months. He hadn't even glanced at it! It didn't seem worth the paper it was written on.

Now I had arrived to start work and was as ready as I'd ever be. It was almost 7.30 am and time I went in.

In my right hand I was clutching a card which had to be handed to the caretaker, and the fingers on my left were half frozen from gripping the handle of my old billycan, containing cold peasoup.

After walking through a tunnel-like central archway, I found myself on a large square playground, flanked on all sides by tall buildings.

Directly opposite me was a wide open door, and I made for that, hoping

158

to find the person in charge of the cleaners.

I had been told to ask for a man named Michael. Apparently he was a Czech and had been given the caretaker's job because he spoke both German and Russian.

There were no signs of any pupils yet, but once inside the school, I came across several adults of varying ages, shapes and sizes; all rushing along endless corridors and up and down wide staircases. Some were in uniform, others wore civilian clothes, and all of them completely ignored me....

Every time I held out my piece of paper, they hurried away as if they thought I was carrying the plague!

I didn't realize that my billycan was giving me away:

I was one of the foreign work force, a piece of German scum! (Yet when this dawned on me, I remembered that they were only reversing the roles! Thinking of the wrongs inflicted on the Russian labour force by my own people, I found it impossible to hate them for the way they treated us chars.)

At long last I found a fat little man in uniform who stopped in his tracks, when I showed him my card, asking:

"Michael?"

He glanced to the left and to the right, making sure we weren't being observed, then beckoned me to follow, uttering just the one word:

"Come!"

I trotted along behind his fast retreating figure until we came to the open door of a small, dark office. The fat little man pointed to it and said:

"Wait!" Then he walked away.

I waited...I was so tense by now that I jumped when the caretaker emerged from a door at the back of the little room. He glanced at my card, looked me up and down and said:

"Good, come with me! I show you work."

I climbed one of the wide staircases after him and thought he didn't seem unfriendly, (more like someone who has a lot on his mind). He was very tall and took rather big strides. I was glad when he paused on the first landing. He pointed up and down the many steps and said:

"You do these twice a day."

I nodded and continued after him, till we came to the top, where he halted in front of a door with the sign: TOILETTEN.

"Other charwoman, she ran off yesterday," he explained," so mess not cleaned up yet... you do mornings, right after children start classes, and after breaks and end of school."

I didn't dare ask why the other woman had run off, seeing it was my first day; but when he opened the door to the cloakroom, I thought I could guess why:

The place was in an undescribable mess! Each cubicle I looked into had everything spattered all over the place, on the walls as well as on the floors....

Michael seemed as disgusted as I was, but he commented that at least part of the fault lay in the peculiar way the Russians constructed their loos....

Apparently one of the first jobs assigned to the press-ganged German artisans had been to adapt the normal toilets to the 'stand above-it' type. They had to build a set of steps for each cubicle as high as the toilet seat, and across this would be fixed a sturdy, wooden platform with a hole in the centre.

The children then climbed onto this contraption and did the necessary....

However, knowing that the hated German women would have to clean up the filth, they did their utmost to make as much mess as they could.

I was appalled at the thought of having to spend a large part of my working day in this hellhole; but not wishing to sound too discouraged, I said:

"I suppose most of the stuff can be swilled down the drains with plenty of water!"

Ignorance really *is* bliss at times!

Until that moment I had taken it for granted there would be at least one drain somewhere in the floor of the cloakroom. I was forgetting that this school was older than the one I'd gone to in Hanover. So it wouldn't come up to the same standards of hygiene!

Michael now looked at me quizzically and asked:

"What drains?"

And when I explained, he flashed his brilliant white teeth at me and laughed:

"No drains here! You scrub — mop into bucket — and pour down toilet!"

Good God! And not a single pair of rubber gloves to be had in all of East Germany!

What about soap powder and disinfectant, I wanted to know. Again he laughed and declared:

"Soap powder not come often. Very short supply.... Russian lady Doctor, she tell women: 'Use more elbow-grease!' She real tartar, you wait and see! She here to-morrow."

Looking back on my time there, it was a good job the woman was elsewhere on my first day, or I might have been too scared to report for work next morning.

As it was, my head was spinning from trying to remember all the different tasks. My lot consisted of two staircases, each with a landing half-way down; and between them stretched a corridor about eighty feet long. The three classrooms on my list had a kind of old fashioned lino-flooring which had to be brushed after sprinkling a tubful of oily sawdust over it. These rooms were only done after the children went home, not like the toilets: Four times a day!

The last place I was shown was a tiny cubby-hole of a room, which belonged to someone called the Inspector. It was to be dusted and tidied only every other day or so.(I shall say more about the Inspector later.)

"Is that all now?" I asked hopefully, when we arrived at the end of my corridor, where it opened into a wide hall, partly filled with coat racks on wheeled frames. Michael shook his dark curls:

"Next job I show you when children get here."

And at that moment there came an almighty blast from the loud speakers, positioned in every corner of the building:

The March of the Toreadors from Carmen! (I cannot listen to that music even now, without being transported back there!)

"Now," he said," is sign children arrived. I make sure you do next job right, then you not get no trouble!"

And then he explained the odd ritual I was to perform twice each day. It was the only part of the work which permitted any kind of contact with the pupils, and was merely due to the fact that the clothes racks were too high for the youngest ones: They couldn't reach the hooks. So I had to help them out of their thick fur coats and hang them up.

However, Michael warned me not to touch these tiny tots in any way! Not to pet them, talk to them, not even to smile at their charming little faces....

"VER-R-R-Y forbidden!" He said and then added a final item to the list of 'Do's and Don'ts':

"When they have break, you put bucket by wall, stand by bucket, hands behind back! Charwomen not move while children play. Top Boss say so!"

All Because Of Him

In all the time I was there I never came across 'Top Boss'.

But I had the feeling that a great many people were afraid of him, and not only the lowly chars. I suspected that he was probably a member of the all-seeing Secret Police, rather than someone in charge of the children's education.

While we were waiting for the youngsters to come upstairs, my mind went back to the previous day, when I was told that I would have to work here....

Having been trained and worked as a Kindergarten teacher, I had thought I might even enjoy some aspects of this job! It would be interesting to observe young people from another nation.

After all, we were no longer at war!

I'd had this optimistic notion that children were children the world over...so I'd make use of my time at the Russian school... an opportunity for some social studies!

"What a daft idea that's turned out to be," I told myself. "Still, I'll be able to watch them! Even with my back to the wall in the literal sense of the word!"

By now a crowd of five-year-olds were assembling by one of the coat racks, all of them were wearing thick fur coats.

And as Michael showed me the exact procedure to follow, I discovered that even these very young ones had been well briefed to avoid contact with us aliens!

They would place themselves in front of me in complete silence, standing there like little furry dolls. First they would lift up their chins to let me undo the top buttons; after that they raised first one arm and then the other, and as soon as they had wriggled out of their sleeves, they dashed off to meet their classmates.

These little ones were charming children, representing the Soviet Union from Europe to Mongolia. I could not help liking them, even though they never raised their eyes to the level of our faces while we were giving them a hand. Sometimes I caught myself hoping for just a tiny smile - but it never happened.

Because of the very cold weather, the tinies did not join the older children in the playground during lunch break. They stayed indoors, playing in the music room or the P.E.-Hall. So the coat ceremony had to be performed only in the morning and after lessons finished.

Buttered Rolls and Belly Pork

It seemed to me that all of mankind's stupidity and inhumanity was symbolised in the silent ritual of the toddlers' furs....

Once the children were in their classrooms, Michael and I went down to the cellar, where he pointed into one of the many recesses and told me that this was the cleaners 'room'.

"You leave coat here, have lunch here, keep gear in corner over there!"

He waited while I hung up my coat and then handed me a bucket, a floor cloth, a scrubbing brush, a broom and a dustpan and brush, and I went up to my landing and set to work.

It was hard, it was disgusting and it was back breaking!

By the time the bell rang for morning break, I felt as though I'd been carrying that bucket for miles....

Up to this point, there had been no hint of trouble, and I felt pleased to have got through the first part. I didn't even mind having to stand with my back to the wall. It felt good to be able to straighten up after all the bending, kneeling and twisting.

But that first part of the morning had been the calm before the storm!

As the pupils were streaming out from their classrooms, the Toreadors started up again, and the first thing that hit me was the din the kids were making!

But they had to compete with the loudspeakers, so I couldn't really blame them.

'My' classrooms housed the older ones. They were between ten and fourteen years old, and their shouting and yelling was deafening. But to begin with it seemed mere exhuberance at having ten minutes of freedom.

Then two of the older girls discovered a new face among the charwomen: ME!

And from that moment on they concentrated on what seemed to be their favourite pastime,(at least during morning break, when they did not go outside): They had invented various games to torment the cleaners, and now I was to have my first sample of them.

To begin with it looked harmless enough.

The two girls who had spotted me were obviously the ringleaders, and as they were passing me, walking arm in arm and giggling like teenagers do, they motioned to their mates to join them....

They all congregated in the far corner of the hall.

I wondered why none of them appeared to be eating the crusty, thickly buttered rolls they'd been given for this break.(I was soon to learn that food was part of their idea of tormenting us.)

The game went like this:

The two leaders, taller than most of the other children and very self-assured and bossy, now made the others form a line.

One of them shouted a command, and the line began to move towards me.

At first I wasn't unduly perturbed.

There was nothing unusual in two strong-willed older children bossing their juniors. I wondered if the two of them were perhaps related to the powerful Top Boss, and thus held in awe by the others?

At the same time I was thinking how pretty most of them were, with their healthy young faces and their shiny hair of all colours and all manner of styles.... They ranged from gold-blond to darkest black, and from short cropped to page boy, as well as intricately beribboned plaits.

And they all, without exception, wore the typical black calf-length boots. (The boots, too, featured frequently in their games in the days that followed.)

So there I stood, wondering what it was all about, asking myself why they were all holding one hand behind their backs, as they were moving slowly and deliberately toward me.... But when they were close enough, I saw the glint in their leader's eyes!

That wasn't childish mischief - it was sheer malice.

Good God! They were children in their early teens!

How was it possible? Then I realized they had been subjected to political indoctrination for much longer than the tiny tots... so what could I expect? The look on their faces made it clear:

There was no way to bridge the gap between us.

As they came closer, they each produced the buttered roll from behind their backs, and my mouth watered at the tempting sight! They knew that the population of East Germany were on starvation rations, whereas the children of Russian soldiers were well fed and didn't really want their snacks....

Once they were face to face with me, each boy or girl took a hearty bite, which made the butter squelch out all around the edges! They gulped down their first bite, waving the delicious roll in front of me,and then they spat on it!

...they each produced the buttered roll from behind their backs...

All Because Of Him

Then they skipped along the corridor and dropped the things into the sink in the corner, turning on the tap to complete the process. All this was accompanied by fiendish laughter, echoing through the hall, together with the music from 'Carmen'.

After they'd gone back to their lessons, I fished out the sodden rolls and carried them down to the cellar, where I had noticed a bin of pig-swill during my round of the building earlier on.

The cellar was a labyrinth of passages and large open areas, as well as numerous locked rooms and crypt-like recesses; and on my way out I noticed a tall soldier leaning against the door frame of one of the rooms.

As I passed him, he made a kind of smacking sound with his lips, which I pretended not to hear. I didn't like the look of him and rushed back upstairs to get on with my jobs.

"I wonder if there's a different way to that pig bin?" I thought. "I must ask the women at lunchtime."

At long last the bell rang, and it was time for an hour's break. I made my way to the recess in the cellar. There were some low wooden benches around the sides, and in one corner stood an ancient boiler.

I learnt later, that this old contraption was supposed to heat the food in our billycans, but it was out of order; and neither we nor our billycans ever derived any warmth or comfort from it.

Lunch was the only time when the women could get together for a smoke and a chat. So now I was to meet them for the first time, and when I arrived in the cellar, there were about ten of them sitting on the hard benches, eating, talking and laughing all at the same time.

Most of them hardly seemed to notice my entrance; and the ones who did return my somewhat timid greeting did so with their mouths full, and went on chatting with their mates....

They all seemed older than I was. Their laughter was caused by one of them regaling her friends with a story of some of her sexual exploits!

My heart sank.

After the encounter with the beastly kids earlier on, I felt a desperate need to talk to a sympathetic listener, but it looked as if these women might have a sort of closed shop as far as I, the outsider, was concerned.

I knew that they would be from an entirely different background to my own. But my first job in Hanover had been with a group of slum children, and I thought I had learnt not to harbour social prejudices....

166

Buttered Rolls and Belly Pork

I certainly didn't wish to be treated any different from the other cleaners!

All I wanted was to be one of the team, because I didn't think I would be able to manage without some moral support.

I squatted down on a half empty bench and started on my cold peasoup, feeling utterly miserable. Every now and then I leaned back against the wall and looked around, trying to find a friendly face among the crowd.

Suddenly, one of the older women smiled at me across the room. I smiled back at her, and she came over and sat down by my side.

"How did you get on during your first morning?" She asked.

"Alright, I suppose." I answered. I knew it didn't sound very convincing, but I wasn't sure what to say about the children.

She went on:

"I suppose you've never worked so hard in your life before! But you'll get used to it."

"It's not the work so much," I told her, "it's the children! How do you cope with those big girls?"

When I told her of the encounter during morning break, she said:

"Yes, that's damned hard! You'll have to grow a thick skin!"

I nodded, feeling useless, spooning away at the congealed soup without appetite. Then I noticed that some of the other women had stopped talking and were regarding me with mild curiosity, until, one by one, they added their own comments about the hate and vindictiveness of the pupils.

"No wonder you're finding it hard," said one, "you've got the worst hellers of the lot on your floor!"

And her neighbour declared:

"Those two ringleaders aren't children, they are devils!"

A vivacious brunette, the one who had been telling them about her sex life, now chimed in:

"But don't let them know they're getting to you! That makes them ten times worse!"

I said meekly, that I had thought I knew about children from my work as a teacher, but that I'd never come across kids like these before.

"Ah, but these brats hate us, an' that's the difference," she sighed and then added with feeling:

"Ignore them! Just think 'to hell with the bastards'!"

"Here, Nelly, mind your language!" An older woman said, and her workmates burst out laughing.

The woman who had first come over to me put her hand on my arm and smiled:

"You can see, we're a rough and ready lot! But don't take any notice, they mean well!"

She told me that she was their spokeswoman, and that her name was Herta. Then she introduced the others to me, but my mind was so full of new impressions, I promptly forgot most of their names.

Nevertheless, I smiled at them all in turn, determined not to mind how they talked or how rough and ready they were, as long as they let me be one of them.

Taken the lead given by Herta, they now began to vie with each other in educating me in the art of cutting corners; and I promised to bear in mind all the tips they gave me, but Herta added a word of caution:

"Mind you don't get caught skimping when the lady doctor is about! She loves to make trouble for us!"

I told them that Michael had already mentioned that one, and then I asked about the fat little man, who had seemed so ill at ease while he was guiding me to Michael's office. Had he been afraid to be seen with me?

"They are all afraid in this place," Herta said,"everybody is in fear of everybody else. No-one wants to be seen doing the wrong thing - such as talking to the likes of us."

"Uh!, what about the soldiers and the officers, then?" Asked the one called Nelly, shaking her auburn curls, " they don't mind being seen with us...and they do a damn sight more than just talk!"

Her last remark caused another outburst of laughter. Some of them hooted at her joke. She was a good looking woman, probably in her early thirties, with a wide sensuous mouth and sparkling hazel eyes. Eyes which gave no clue to the hardships of her life.

But for me, her hint at what went on with the military personnel had now introduced a new note of alarm!

I guessed that their functions as guards, drivers and managers of provisions made them play an important part behind the scenes.

But because I was still quite a prude, and I was scared, I thought:

"I mustn't get too close to her! I don't want to get involved with the soldiers, especially if it means 'more than just talking'!"

Yet I should have liked to ask some questions about the men who frequented the cellars, about who was dangerous, and who was alright...but we had only just become pals. It might have seemed I was prying....

The bell interrupted my thoughts.

Everybody got up to return to the treadmill, and I was about to follow them, when Herta got hold of my arm and said:

"Hang on a minute."

She waited till the others were out of earshot and went on:

"There's something you ought to know, but I want to tell you while we are by ourselves."

I looked at her care-worn face, thinking she might be old enough to be my mother, and waited for her to continue:

"You'll see some of the officers in here during lunch on most days. But you mustn't pay any attention to them! Don't look at them, don't laugh at what they get up to! Pretend you are a bit dim or something, then they'll leave you alone."

I could only stare at her, and she smiled indulgently:

"You really are rather green...how old are you?"

"Twenty-three," I answered, thinking that in spite of some of the hair-raising encounters with the occupying forces during the past two years, I was still incredibly naive!

She nodded.

"I thought you couldn't be much more than that. So you are the youngest one here." After a moment's hesitation she added:

"Are you married?"

"Yes." My answer came without enthusiasm, which I was hoping she wouldn't detect. The unhappy state of affairs at home had nothing to do with my work here...and I didn't wish to talk about it....

I didn't want anyone to know that the time for saving my marriage was running out fast.

Herta couldn't have noticed, though, because she returned to the subect of the officers:

"You will soon see that several of the women have their regular patrons among the officers. So if you don't encourage them, you'll have nothing to fear."

I nodded numbly. And she added:

"The only one to be afraid of is the tall one in charge of the stores. His room is in the cellar."

All Because Of Him

I suddenly remembered the soldier I had seen standing in the doorway down there. I said:

"Oh, I've met him when I was going to the pig-bin."

Herta stuck out her lower lip and blew a sigh of mock protest up to the wispy bits of grey hair, fluttering above her forehead:

"God almighty!" She groaned, "don't you ever go down there on your own again! Just tip the rolls down the toilet!"

"But he never touched me!"

"Well, that's a miracle!" She shook her head, picked up her bucket, saying it was time we got back to work, and we walked towards the stairs.

But I was still battling with the question about the women and the soldiers! I couldn't understand how anyone could submit to them willingly, even treat the whole thing as a joke!

(It hadn't occurred to me at the time that unless they treated all life as a joke, some of them wouldn't have been able to bear it.) So I said:

"But how can the women have sex with those men? I think that's terrible!"

She stopped in her tracks, and I realized I'd made a mistake: It was the comment of an ignorant female, who'd had a sheltered upbringing!

"There you are," she said, "that's why I didn't want to speak to you about it in front of the others!"

"I don't understand! Don't their husbands mind? And what about their children?"

She looked at me steadily, and her reply made me feel ashamed at my lack of insight.

"Yes," she said, "what about their husbands? What about their children? Some of these women don't know if their men are alive or dead; and their children cry themselves to sleep at night, because they're hungry!"

I was listening to her without a word. She went on:

"They don't go with the soldiers for nothing, you know! They get paid with extra rations....You mustn't forget: High morals don't feed empty bellies!"

"I'm sorry," was all I could say, and with that we parted to get to our seperate work areas.

The afternoon dragged on, and at last it was time to go home. I noticed that all my new workmates were in a tearing hurry to stash away their gear, put on their coats and get out of the cellar. They told me that they had

Buttered Rolls and Belly Pork

developed a special procedure for their exit on the days when the tall soldier was in his lair: They stayed close together like a flock of sheep, all pushing in unison towards the doors....

And they made sure I wasn't left behind!

That first evening, I decided not to be beaten:

Not by the hard work or the hateful children, not by the lecherous bloke in the cellar or the forbidding lady doctor, who was looming on to-morrow's horizon....

That resolution got a big dent early the next morning before I'd even got out of bed. I felt so stiff, I didn't think I could wield that broom or get down on my knees....

And after I got up, I discovered that a new layer of snow had fallen overnight, which would mean a long trudge through the city.

Trams wouldn't be able to run.

However, I got there, and Herta was waiting for me.

She wanted a quick word, while I hung up my coat and got my equipment.

"Sorry, if I spoke too harshly yesterday," she whispered," I had to tell you, so you didn't get on your high horse in front of the others!"

"That's alright!" I said, "I know I was wrong!"

"You'd lose their good will, if they felt you were judging them!"

"Thanks for the warning, anyway!" It was good to know she cared!

She winked at me and grinned:

"Just think of their capers as a quick fix in a broom cupboard!"

I had to laugh. She had cheered me up so much; I even imagined I was ready for whatever the day might bring, when one of the others, who had already been upstairs, came back and told us to hurry up:

The Doctora had already been seen on the prowl!

So my feeling of euphoria began to evaporate before I'd even reached my own section!

And after morning break it vanished altogether, because when I left my place against the wall, to go and do the cloakrooms, I discovered that the children had stuffed the buttered rolls so tightly into the sink, that the water had overflowed and flooded that part of the hall!

Blast!

After I'd cleared the sink and mopped up, I was late for the toilets. So I skimped a bit here and there, hoping that it wouldn't be noticed....

All Because Of Him

But that was a mistake:

Back on my knees in the corridor, I became aware that someone was watching me. I looked up and there stood a full-busted woman with grey-blond hair. It was plaited around a fleshy face; and from this face her steel-grey eyes were blazing at me angrily:

Madame Doctora!

She motioned to me to get up and snarled:

"Toiletten!"

She'd been checking up on the newcomer and had found the morning's weak spot.

"Do again!" She hissed and stomped along ahead of me...and when we got there, she stood watching over my efforts, while I did a more thorough job.

When it was done, I rushed back to get on with the hall, and within minutes she was there again, scrutinizing every inch of the cream-coloured tiles....

Suddenly she spat on her finger, bent down and started rubbing vigorously at one of them. Then she straightened up, pointed to a slightly lighter patch where she'd been rubbing, and demanded:

"There! You get all floor like that!"

Frustration and anger were beginning to boil over inside me.... What did she think we could achieve with no soap-powder and only ice-cold water?

And I told her so!

Most Russians could speak and understand a fair amount of German, so I was sure the lady knew what I was saying. And in case she really didn't get my drift, I added a little mime, showing the way one sprinkles powder onto the floor....

She gave a derisive snort and patted her elbow, saying something in Russian, which probably was their word for elbowgrease. It made me think of Michael's warning. He had been right: The woman was a 'Proper Tartar'!

"Use more this!" She said, still patting her fat elbow, but by now I'd had enough and merely shrugged my shoulders, staring back at her gimletty eyes.

That was the moment the bell announced the lunch break, and who should be first to emerge from the older pupils' classroom but my two chief adversaries!

Buttered Rolls and Belly Pork

They slowed their steps as they passed the Doctora confronting the char-woman, just in time to hear her parting shot:

"Deutsche Frau: Nix Cultura! Deutsche Frau: Nix Hygiena!"

She marched off, and the two girls disappeared round the corner on their way to the dining room.

Seen from where I stood, they could have been two normal teenagers, putting their heads together, sharing a joke or a secret: One with short, free-flowing, jet black hair, the other with long blond plaits, entwined with coloured ribbons, trailing all the way down her back....

It was what went on inside those pretty heads, which made these two unlike most other youngsters. I had no doubt they were hatching another plot.

When I arrived in our quarters in the cellar, Herta was again waiting for me. She had been wondering what had made me late.

"You alright?" She asked.

I nodded, grateful for her concern, but too full of mixed emotions to speak. I was afraid I might burst into tears, if I let myself go.

The anger and resentment against the Doctora's interference were chok-ing me. There was the dread of whatever the girls were planning for their next assault; and as if that wasn't enough, I had just seen several of the uniformed personnel waiting about in the cellar passage. The doors along it had stood open, and, passing them, I had wondered, if this was in prepara-tion for their special lunch time activities?

I didn't have to wait long to find out....

By the time all the cleaners had arrived for their hour's respite, several of the men had also drifted into our recess. They sat down next to some of the younger women, who clearly were on familiar terms with them. They used sign language most of the time, accompanied by a good deal of nudg-ing and prodding!

Herta, who had wisely taken the space next to me on the seat, now said under her breath:

"Remember: Don't get involved!"

"O.K." I whispered. I was going to behave like the three wise monkeys.

After a few minutes of banter and loud laughter, some of the men got up and left. I looked at Herta and she explained:

"They're going back on duty. They only came in to sort out details for a meeting tonight."

All Because Of Him

I suppose my face must have looked as if she'd spoken to me in a foreign tongue, which made her say:

"You just keep looking like you do now, and you'll be safe as houses! But if you must know: Yes they do have orgies some nights, and that's all I know! I haven't been to any!"

I continued eating my lentils without another word.

After a while there was only one young officer left, and he was sitting next to Nelly.

Suddenly he jumped to his feet and bent over her, crooked one arm round her neck and ordered:

"Come!"

He yanked her to her feet and she squealed in mock protest; but her movements were not like those you'd expect from a maiden in distress.... We could hear her shrieking and laughing as he led her along one of the passages and into his den.

The other women went on eating their lunch without batting an eyelid. They were carrying on a detailed discussion about who got killed in the last few air-raids of the war. Apparently some of them had helped to dig out their own relatives.

"What a sight that was," gloated a plump young woman, waving her spoon about, "If it hadn't been my mother-in-law, I would have felt sorry! All to pieces and her insides hanging out! But she'd been an old witch, I was glad she was dead!"

There were more descriptions of similar nature, so I put the lid firmly onto my billycan: I'd lost my appetite and hoped my stomach would keep down what I'd eaten.... It did. And that was something to be grateful for!

It was not long before Nelly returned.

She was clutching two brown paper parcels to her chest. From the end of one of them protruded a sizeable piece of belly pork, and we were told that the other one contained a lump of butter 'as big as a cabbage'. She proudly displayed her trophies to the rest of us.

"There you are," she laughed as if she had just come back from a shopping trip, "I haven't been long, have I?"

The women looked at her bounty admiringly, without any apparent envy. They knew there were four growing youngsters in Nellie's family....And some of them commented drily that it would be their turn tonight!

"Yea!" Nelly retorted," I bet you won't better this, though! Mind you, it

174

was a damn rough job! But it was worth it!"

And then they all fell about laughing!

That was my introduction to the activities that went on below ground on most days.

During that afternoon, when everything seemed quiet, the bullygirls found an excuse to leave their classroom.

They made a point of examining my tiles, wagging their heads this way and that, like they had seen the Doctora do....What were they up to now?

Oh, the craftiness of them!

They knew that the cleaners were to scrub only half the width of the long corridor at any one time, making sure there would always be one length dry enough to walk on without slipping. So when they had discovered which part was wet, they proceeded to dance along that section right to the end of the corridor: And as they did so, they rubbed their black heels, criss-cross fashion, on each clean tile!

It really was *very* hard not to hate them! Them and their black Russian boots!

The first two days had been a fair sample of what to expect on a normal day. There were variations, of course, such as when the Doctora was absent, so we didn't have to expect her appearing from behind doors and around corners. And there were a few days when the big girls were away on a break with their families.

The adult population of the school continued to ignore us, apart from one teacher who sometimes held open a door for me, when I was carrying a bucket of water,(but only when no-one was in sight).

Apart from him, the only other Russian who treated me (almost) like another human being was the Inspector. But he also gave me a big fright during my first week there, and it happened like this:

When I went to clean his small office for the first time, he turned out to be the fat little man who had helped me to locate Michael on my first morning as a char.

I had popped my head around his door, showing him my broom and duster, raising my eyebrows in a sort of "Alright-now?" motion; in answer to which he'd waved me away, saying:

"Tomor-r-r-ow!"

Well, that suited me fine. I'd have more time for the other chores.

When 'Tomorrrow' came, I decided to leave his place until last thing before lunch. It would only need a quick sweep and a flick with the duster.

So I knocked at his door. He let me in, and I set to work, while he went in and out of the room on various errands. I paid no attention to his comings and goings, and he seemed quite oblivious of my presence there.

By the time I had finished, he had disappeared once again. I picked up my things and went to the door. I turned the handle:

It was locked!

There was a moment of shock and disbelief, and then the feeling of being let down: I had not expected it from the fat little man!

When I began to take stock of my predicament, I wondered whether there might be a way out other than the door: I went to the window, maybe I could jump out. But I was on the second floor of a building with very high rooms; and, apart from that, I found that the catch had been broken, and the window was nailed up.

There was a small cupboard at waist level, which I knew to be accessible from the adjoining classroom. It was closed on the far side by a large blackboard, which moved up and down on a sash.

The classroom was empty at the time, because the pupils were having a music lesson, so I thought I'd climb through....

But however hard I tried to heave up the heavy board, my fingers couldn't get a hold on its smooth surface.

It was impossible to shift it, and after I had broken two fingernails, I gave up trying.

Well, if I couldn't get out, I'd better think of some means of defending my honour!

There was my broom....I could clout him over the head with that, if the worst came to the worst.

"The main thing is, not to panic!" I told myself, thinking of the many other times when I'd been in a tight spot with members of the Red Army. I remembered how I'd always got away with no more than a big fright, always followed by a feeling of overwhelming relief, when I found myself still in one piece!

I knew that all those encounters had had one thing in common:

Each time I'd been saved by the fact that I'd been able to appear calm and unruffled, no matter how shaky I might be feeling inside....

So I sent a quick prayer skywards, asking for the degree of calmness necessary, and then settled myself on the Inspector's desk to wait. (I had decided on the desk rather than his comfortable chair, because it would be quicker to get into un upright position that way!)

And I waited.

It seemed ages, but it was really no more than twenty minutes or so, and all the while I kept telling myself to remain cool!

I found myself wondering Herta hadn't warned me about him. After all, she had worked here for a long time, she knew all the hazards of the job!

At last I heard the key being turned in the lock.

I jumped off the desk, ready for battle to commence!

And I'll never know who looked sillier during the next few moments:

The fat little man, who blinked his eyes as if he was seeing a ghost, when he discovered I was still there... or I, when I had to re-arrange my face...because the way I had been glaring at him had said plainly:

"You dare, you old devil!"

But it was quite obvious that he had completely forgotten about the charwoman in his office! And as soon as he realized his mistake, the look on his round pug face went from astonishment to an apologetic grin... and then he tapped his head as if to say he'd been an ass....

So I just smiled at him.

He turned and held open the door for me and then stood aside, while I clattered past him with my bucket and broom and all.

What an anti-climax!

I couldn't wait to tell Herta and the others! They were half way through their lunch, when I got to the cellar.

"Where have YOU been?" Herta asked. "We were getting worried!"

"Not half as worried as I was until a few minutes ago!"

I told them my tale, and they all thought it was hilarious, especially Nelly. She joked:

"As long as you only get locked in by the Ispector, you're alright! You won't get any belly pork, but you won't loose your precious virtue either!"

More laughter.

Then I noticed that some of the women were missing:

Forgetting Herta's advice, I asked:

"Where are the others?"

Still more laughter. All except Herta who gave me a dig in the ribs and said:

"Now remember: Mind your own business!"

All Because Of Him

Whereupon Nelly turned on me in mock-reproach and, wagging her finger at me, said sternly:

"Don't ask no silly questions, and you'll be told no lies... but seeing you're now one of us, I'll tell you: The others are on an early assignment."

And now they were all rocking with hoots and shrieks at her account of what went on behind the closed doors of the cellar passages....

"Oh, Nelly!" I thought, wishing with all my heart that I could feel easier about their capers in broom cupboards, their orgies and their assignments. It wasn't prejudice on my part now. No, I was sad about the plight of them all. Yet there was nothing I could do. They had accepted their lot and were making the best of it. So who was I, to play Cassandra, warning them about the risks?

No, I'd just have to laugh with them and say nothing.

Of course, they were aware of the risks! But like so many people during those early post-war days, they probably felt the present was all they could think of! If there was a future, it would take care of itself. NOW was the time we had to live through....

Days went by and turned into weeks, filled with the same chores, marked by the same frustrations and humiliations...but, for me, all made bearable through the fellowship of the other women.

During the fourth week, I developed a severe cold.

After coughing all night, I felt exhausted before I even got half way through the first part of each morning. And it seemed as if my chief persecutors had a sixth sense: They were particularly trying all week.

And, to top it all, the tall soldier in the cellar had begun to cast his eyes in my direction!

On the Monday, I'd had to ask him for a new broom. The handle on mine had snapped. Bearing in mind Herta's warning, I had asked one of the older women to go to the store room with me.

Everything seemed alright. He wasn't even smelling of drink, when he handed me the replacement... but when we turned away, he put his hand on my shoulder and said:

"You clean my room for me, yes?"

I shook my head, shrugged of his hand and left him standing there. I mumbled something about being in a hurry, and my chaperon and I rushed upstairs.

It had seemed easier than I had expected, and I was hoping he might take 'No' for an answer, which turned out to be a false hope!

Because since then he had been standing in his doorway whenever we had entered the cellar, saying something to me as I passed him. It was becoming more and more difficult to pretend I hadn't heard.

But all my workmates were aware of the situation; and Herta now kept a close eye on me. She explained about his tactics:

He would single out one of the women and tell her to sweep his store room at the end of the day. The woman thus chosen would pretend to agree, would say:

"Later," or "maybe!"

Some of them had had to fight him off tooth and nail, so they had developed their own strategy. And now, whenever he was waiting for one of us to be caught, the women would form a kind of human wall around the 'Intended' and make a wild dash for the exit.

But he was beginning to get wise to their schemes and would try to halt the stampede as they pressed past him, shouting at them to stop!

A week or so ago, after one of these hurried exits, Herta had reassured me:

"He has no right to order us about, quite apart from the other thing! If he starts on you, let me know!"

And now I was hoping that the other women would re-enact the desperate getaway for me as well!

My cold was getting worse. I was feeling so wretched, I remember flattening my back as tightly as I could against the ice cold outside wall during breaktime, hoping I'd develop pneumonia! That would stop me working in the miserable place!

On the Thursday of that week the children flooded part of my hall first thing in the morning, before they'd even began their lessons. They'd stuffed the sink with pieces of paper and turned the tap on as full as possible; so when I came back from doing the toilets the place was well and truly awash!

I dragged myself through the day, and towards the end of the afternoon, as an extra bonus, the Inspector forgot once again that I was still in his room and locked me in....

But this time I wasn't worried.

I knew he didn't mean any harm. I could also hear voices in the adjacent classroom, so I opened the wall cupboard, knocked on the backboard on its far side and waited.

All Because Of Him

Of course, among the pupils having a lesson beyond it were the two bullies, but that couldn't be helped...I was relieved to see that the teacher who pushed up the heavy blackboard was the one who had sometimes held open the door to me.

He now peered at me through the dark aperture, and I conveyed my predicament to him by hand signals. He stood back and waited for me to scramble over dusty bottles and jars, broken rulers and bits of loose chalk. I must have looked a sight when I emerged!

I nodded a quick 'Thankyou!' and he pulled down the board again, while his class burst into mirthless jeering laughter as I hastened out into the corridor.

By the time the bell rang to announce the end of school, I had decided to do the rest of today's chores, like the loos and the classrooms, with as little effort as possible!

I would do a more thorough job in the morning, if I hadn't got pneumonia by then....

So after I'd helped the tinies with their coats, I walked back to start on the classrooms. Coming closer to the bully girls' room, I heard the most infernal din emerging from its open door....

My spirits flagged!

Please, God, no extra trouble now! I was so very tired, I could hardly carry the bucket....

What were they doing in there anyway? They were supposed to have left at the same time as the teacher!

When I arrived at their door, I saw what it was all about:

They had torn their exercise books into hundreds and hundreds of small pieces the size of tiddlywinks. Some of them were still at it, making piles of the stuff on the top of their desks.

One of the leaders saw me and gave a shout....

It must have been the signal to start: They gathered a handful at a time and scattered the bits into the air, it was a real paper snowstorm. The little white segments whirled about and dropped onto the floor, onto the stupid lino, which was always so sticky because of the oily sawdust....

I thought:

"If only I were the type of woman who can faint at times like this!"

But then, what good would fainting do?

And, in spite of all my principles, I DID hate those teenagers as they jostled past me to get through the door, leaving me to pick up the pieces.

They raced along the hall to get to their coats,yelling their heads off about their latest triumph!

It took ages to pick up the scraps clinging to the lino.

No broom could cope with that!

A broom could catch the few bits lying on top, but there were thousands of pieces to be picked up by hand!

Crawling about on my knees, I was sure Cinderella'd had a cushy job compared to mine....

Herta popped her head in at the door and said:

"Blast those brats!"

I looked up at her, feeling helpless and hopeless, and she said soothingly:

"I'll do the toilets! I've skipped one of my rooms, and Nelly'll be up in a minute and give you a hand!"

"I haven't done the other two rooms yet!"

But Herta had decided that we wouldn't have time:

"We'll skip those, because HE's hanging about the exit. We must all get out together!"

When we got to the cellars, the tall soldier strode up to me and said:

"You clean my room for me now, yes?"

I shook my head:

"Too late today! Tomorrow!"

He mocked:

"Tomorrow! Tomorrow, you no more say 'later',! Tomorrow you DO!"

He spat on the floor and left.

One more day's grace....

Then it was Friday, and I still hadn't got pneumonia!

There was nothing for it but to brazen it out, however ghastly I felt. And, partly because of the state I was in, the morning seemed more fraught with hazards than ever!

The cloakrooms were in a terrible mess after each break;and the fat lady Doctor was acting like a Jack in the box, popping up here, there and everywhere!

Then there was a smell of gas on my floor.

It must have been very strong, seeing that I had noticed it in spite of my stuffy nose! I fetched Michael, we located the source of the smell: It came from the big lab-room, around the corner from my hall....He got out his master key and we entered the lab.

One of the taps had been turned on!

I rushed across the room to open the windows, while Michael turned off the gas and checked all the appliances, swearing and cursing in his mother tongue....

He growled:

"This room locked all time... but boys crawl in through cupboard in wall!"

I remembered my own recent effort at climbing through one of the cupboards: It hadn't been fun for me, but I could understand the attraction it would have for young boys!

However, turning the gas on was a different matter!

Michael hadn't finished yet:

"I no hate Germans! But I wish Russian kids go to hell! AND their soldiers!"

I felt like adding the Doctora to his list, but I took it for granted that she was included!

The weather had turned bitterly cold even for a German winter, so it had been decided that the older pupils were to stay in during lunch break, as well as the tinies. We could hear them running and shouting above our heads, while we were having our rest in the cellar.

After we'd finished our soup, Herta suggested she and I had better go upstairs to avoid the storeman, should he appear...but we were too late!

He sauntered in to remind me that he would be waiting, and to my horror, I could smell Whisky from right across the recess....

The drink seemed to make him more belligerent, because he came close to my face and said:

"No more 'Later'! Today, you clean my cellar!"

And now it was no use telling myself that he had no authority to ask us to work for him, or to threaten and bully us....

There was no-one we could have turned to! Michael had no power to prevent the soldiers from doing anything they wished.

I was shivering, partly from my cold, and partly from the chilly drafty room, but mostly from fear....

So once the storekeeper had turned away and left, Herta pulled me to my feet and led me up to the floor above, where we would be away from

Buttered Rolls and Belly Pork

him.

The children had by now all gone to their favourite indoor areas where they would spend the rest of the lunch hour. Some were in the big gymnastics hall, others went to read in the library, but most of them had assembled in the large, lofty music room on the first floor.

The cleaners were not to go near there, when the children were in it, but Herta pulled me into one of the deep, empty recesses in the wall opposite the double doors. These niches would have housed life-size busts of famous people in bygone days. No-one would notice us there.

Herta said:

"I thought you needed cheering up: Listen!"

I listened.

We had heard a noise of clapping and cheering, as we came up the stairs. Standing in our niche we could see the beautifully polished grand piano: But I couldn't see who had been playing. Then I noticed a pair of short, black-booted legs dangling from the piano stool...one of the tinies, 'my' five-year-olds! Too small to be seen above the open lid, too short to reach the pedals, but not too young to play a charming Russian folksong!

I was struck by the atmosphere in that room.

It was the first time I had ever seen the children in their true light, away from indoctrination or spite.

There in that music room, all that was natural, happy and child-like came into its own for a short while....

After the invisible little one had finished her recital and sliped off the stool, some of the older boys and girls took turns at the Bechstein, and I marvelled at their skill: They were playing marches, Russian folkdances and waltzes.

The piano had come to life!

And once the dance music had started, both teen-agers and toddlers danced around the room in happy abandon....

Herta and I stood watching, completely captivated by the scene. I even forgot the man in the cellar... and the lines from the Merchant of Venice came to my mind, the ones about the man that 'Hath no music in himself....

Oh, but these children had so much talent!

They were glowing with the joy of the lovely melodies filling the place! And yet we knew: Had they discovered us, they could have turned into little furies in an instant!

All Because Of him

Why did there have to be so much hate?

Herta looked at her watch. She whispered:

"The bell's going to ring in a minute. Let's go before they see us!"

So we made our way towards the stairs, loath to break the spell. Before we parted, she said:

"Don't worry about him in the cellar! We'll get you out by hook or by crook!"

The Doctora must have had the afternoon off, which was a relief. No-one noticed, how I hurried through the chores. I was literally praying on my knees, scouring the beastly tiles.

My mind seemed to go round in circles, in time with the movement of the scrubbing brush...while the clock at the end of the hall was telling me to hurry, hurry, hurry!

I must be ready for whatever Herta and the others were planning!

At last I had finished the classrooms and toilets, (and be damned to the bits I'd missed!).

As I picked up my gear to go down the stairs, my knees felt as if they were no part of me, and my mouth was so dry, it felt like sandpaper....But then I got to the top of the stairs, and I forgot about my tired, aching limbs:

All the women were trouping up to meet me, with Herta a few steps ahead of them!

"Wait there." She said, and from behind her stepped Nelly, pulling my coat out from under her imitation fur jacket.

"Quick! Put it on NOW! So you won't need to go into the cellar!"

One of the others then pulled out my billycan from inside her overall. She'd wrapped my headscarf about it, to make it look round, matching her bosom!

Struggling to get into my coatsleeves, I asked:

"Is he there?"

"Yes," said Herta, "and he's drunk!"

I tied on my scarf, and Nelly pulled it forward to hide most of my face. Then all of them moved around me, forming a tight circle.

"Right!" Said Herta,"all together now - and if he tries to stop us, push him over! GO!"

How did we ever manage to get down those flights of stairs without anyone tripping and bringing us all to the bottom in one big heap?

It was sheer mad desperation, but it worked!

Buttered Rolls and belly Pork

The drunken soldier was waiting at the entrance to the cellar steps, and when he saw us, he realized he was about to be cheated once again!

He gave a shout, raised his arms and tried to flail his way into the bunch of tightly knit females, who were all pressing towards the exit....

But none of them gave way!

I felt like a potato on a conveyor belt, joggled along by all the other potatoes....

And then, somehow, I was pushed through the big open doors, and as I tumbled into the snowy playground, they all shouted:

"RUN!"

I ran alright!

I raced across that square, as if I had the devil after me.... His enraged bellowing echoed around the enclosing walls!

By the time I was half-way across the square, my breath was coming in gasps, steaming in the freezing air. I was making for the large tunnel of the main archway, and was telling my legs to keep going!

I could see glimpses of normal life passing by the end of that tunnel: People walking and a tram rattling along....

Now I'd reached the dark passage and was about to slacken my pace, to give my bursting lungs a chance to draw a deep breath....

But then there was a sort of sharp cracking noise...twice, and then the clatter of falling bits of masonry, as two shots hit the wall behind me....

I don't remeber how I got home.

But when I finally stopped shivering that night, I decided that enough was enough: I would go to visit my people in the West!

Yes, that was IT: I would go with or without my wavering husband....(It would be a sort of 'Final Test', as far as our marriage was concerned!)

The trek to the other side of No-man's-land' would be fraught with dangers. But at least, once I'd crossed the border, there would be no more spiteful Doctora, no drunken soldier and no more children tormenting me with their buttered rolls!

But I knew I should miss the women, especially Herta's kindness; and, of course, Nelly, with her sense of fun and her arms full of belly-pork....

The Applekeeper

I NEVER knew the name of the old man who helped us to get away, nor did I ever learn the names of the people who were part of the venture. It was safer not to know.

There was no time for formalities: We met, accepted each other's risks and each other's comradeship... and afterwards we parted.

It was Septmeber 1948. The month had begun with days of unblemished sunshine after misty mornings and clear starlit nights. It would be just right for the trip, I thought, sitting in the dingy waiting room of the half-derelict station, watching people come and go.

Until the end of the war this place had been merely a little known stop somewhere between Magdeburg and Hanover. Only branch line trains called here, puffing their way from village to village, providing the only link for most of the population between neighbouring hamlets and the city.

These days, however, the small halt had acquired a significance undreamt of until a couple of years ago: It was the end of the line between East and West-Germany. A few miles from the adjoining village was No-Man's-Land; and beyond that, for the people living in the East, lay another world: For them the West was out of bounds!

Noisy, worn-out engines were dragging dilapidated carriages to and from this place. They would break down in the middle of nowhere as often as not, which would mean long delays all along the line, because the new Russian authorities, in their 'wisdom', had removed all the second tracks here. So if *one* engine was stuck, everything was stuck!

The cargo the ancient carriages were taking on and spewing out consisted of a few paltry goods sent to markets and shops, and the passengers were mainly farmers and housewives, intent on their everyday business.

One had to look closely at them to dicover a few men and women who wouldn't fit into these categories, even though they might try to appear just like the rest of the locals....

186

The Applekeeper

They were the ones I'd been waiting for: Like myself, for one reason or another, they wanted to make the perilous trek into the West; and I was hoping to pick out a safe travelling companion from among them.

The driver of a ramshackle lorry had given me a lift from the outskirts of Magdeburg. He'd set me down a mile or so away from here, and I had made my way to the station.

The whistle of the three o'clock train now announced its imminent departure back to the town... and I remembered that there was only one more train today. After that the crowd, now standing about or sitting on hard wooden benches, would disperse. Even the old farmers, who seemed to treat the place as a sort of clubroom, would wander off home; and I would find myself stuck here! The room was probably locked at night....

It was high time to find someone who looked honest enough and strong enough to join me on the long march.

I had made the trip several times in the past two years, visiting my parents in Hanover. Recently, though, the conditions in the border country were becoming more and more fraught with danger; and last time, when I had travelled on my own, it had been too gruelling an experience for me to dare repeat it....

Perched on the hard seat, clutching my hold-all on my knees, surrounded by smoking, chatting, coughing or sleeping men and women, I looked about me: The walls were of a dirty yellow with torn posters still adhering to the flaking paint. Large patches of damp showed where the rains had found their way through the roof; and the crumbling plaster of the ceiling sprouted irregular patterns of black, green and yellow mould.

Everything looked ugly and depressing, and I thought:

"Maybe it's the apprehension before the ordeal, which is making me feel so gloomy! Or perhaps it's the knowledge that I've burnt my boats?"

But it was best not to dwell on that now: The reason for this last and final trek to the West, the broken marriage, the dreams which had come to nothing - this was not the time to think about it.

The only thing that mattered now, was to find the right person, and I was hoping that somewhere among this crowd of people, there would be a woman, who would fit the bill! But from where I sat, I could only see a few of the people clearly, partly because of the smoky atmosphere, and partly because a cluster of old men. They were taking up the space in the middle of the room, their talk interrupted by puffs from their pipes, while they were attempting to set the world to rights....

I decided it would only draw attention to myself, if I were to walk about inspecting everybody. I'd just have to wait.

But oh, it was dreary in here!

My spirits didn't rise either, when I remembered some of the stories circulating about this border area: The talk of false guides, who were said to operate from places like this station. They offered to take people across for large sums of money... then delivered them into the hands of the feared and hated People's Police, pocketing a reward for their treachery....

There were also rumours of fugitives being shot at, or being robbed and killed for a few belongings...and some had even been dragged back by border patrols, when they'd already crossed to the other side and thought they were safe!

"Still," I told myself," with the right timing and a good bit of luck, it should be alright."

As yet there were no electric fences or watch towers in this neighbourhood. The most important condition for a safe crossing would be the direction of the wind just before dawn; because at one stage one had to pass within sight of some Police barracks, and adjoining them were their tracker dogs kennels....

Then I thought of the secret path through the forest, which in by-gone days had been used by courting couples and berry-pickers. Recently, though,the entrance to it had become rather overgrown by bramble thickets and remained only as a dark hollow in the undergrowth.

If all went well, this little winding way would lead the traveller to the dual-carriage way: The Autobahn in the British Sector.

My thoughts were interrupted by some noisy laughter and cheerful good-byes from some of the old men, who were beginning to drift from the room into the late afternnon sunshine outside. Once they'd gone, I had a clear space in front of me, and I noticed a woman in a plain summer frock on the seat opposite.

Her mid-brown hair was partly covered by a faded scarf. She wore no make-up, nothing to attract a second glance. Most women at that time didn't want to invite unwelcome attentions from Russian soldiers, so female attire tended to be on the drab side.

She was wearing sturdy lace-up shoes. They were still quite clean: It was unlikely that she'd been on a shopping trip in town: They were shoes you'd wear for a long walk!

I also noticed that, like myself, she only had a small holdall on her knees. It looked just roomy enough to carry a few necessities and food to last for the journey. Of course, it was meant to appear as if it contained a day's shopping....

"I wonder if she's strong enough," I mused, looking at her slender hands, which were gripping her bag nervously. They were well-kept hands and certainly had not been used to hard work.

"Still, she's got a nice open face," I continued my deliberations, knowing that any moment now it would be time to put my cards on the table.

I smiled across at her, tentatively at first, and when she smiled back, I nodded, as if I'd just noticed an old acquaintance. She picked up the light coat lying by her side and moved over on the bench to make room for me.

I got up, walked over to her and sat down. Had I found my companion?

The first few words we spoke were as tentative as our smiles had been: About having spent a pleasant morning, and about having a rest before going on up the road... and how there was nothing much in the shops these days...all quite casual and non-committal.

I thought her voice sounded pleasant, even though her bearing showed the tension she felt. Her fingers kept on tightening and loosening on the handles of her grip, and her feet were tucked in tightly beneath the seat. She looked as if she wished to melt away.

I thought: "I'd better come to the point, she might feel better once things are open between us," so I asked:

"Are you going my way? It would be nice to have company, wouldn't it?" I had chosen my words carefully to leave her a way out, but I felt sure that she knew what lay behind my questions.

And she understood! Her eyes lit up and she breathed a sigh of relief:

"Yes, please! Let's walk back together!" This, too, was said as if we were going no further than the end of the village...but we both knew....

From then on we kept up the pretence of being old friends, but we were now discussing the way ahead with its pitfalls and loopholes. We discovered that we both knew of the same secret path, and though she admitted she was scared, she said she was determined to make the trip.

I wondered fleetingly what could have set her on this road, but now was not the time to ask. If she wanted to talk about it, there would be time enough later in the night, after we'd found a place to hide before the last lap.

"Let's wait here a little longer," I said, "because it's no use getting close to the forest in the evening, when the patrols can spot us from miles away."

She agreed.

We would leave the station presently and stroll along the road in a leisurely fashion, until we were out of sight of the village. Then we'd walk for a few miles in a Westerly direction till we found somewhere to shelter, some place still far enough from the reaches of the patrols roaming across No-man's-land. And then some time in the small hours, we would set out on the final and most perilous part of the journey. But we could talk about all that later....

I thought I should warn her about the kind of resting place we might find, though, it would save disappointment later on, so I said:

"We might not find a barn or anything like that, but it's been a warm day, so may be a copse somewhere will do."

"I've never spent a night in the open, not even in a tent," she sighed, "but we'll have to take what comes."

I smiled at her:

"Don't worry about it yet! Once we get into our stride, you might even enjoy the walk!"

"Oh, I'm not worried about the first part!" She said, "we'll be just two women coming back from a trip to town...it's after we get to the places with no signs of life that it's going to be creepy!"

In an attempt to make her feel more at ease, I joked:

"You just wait till we get out there, and you'll be praying that there's no sign of life for miles!"

She smiled ruefully, and we stopped talking for a while.

Suddenly, a young boy slipped into the room and eyed the handful of people still gathered there like a fox entering a chicken run, trying to decide which old hen to make for....

After a few moments' survey, he ambled over to where the woman and I were sitting.

He planted himself in front of us and said with a disarming smile:

"Hello, Aunties! I've arrived!"

He waited for a few seconds to let his words sink in, and then he continued:

"Thanks for meeting me here! It's ages since I've been in the village, so

The Applekeeper

I'm not sure about the way to your place."

Well!

What could we say?

His game of 'Let's pretend' was ingenious, to say the least; and he certainly was playing his part well...so well in fact that I wondered about his sincerety to begin with....

Should we enter into the spirit of it, or pretend we hadn't got the meaning of his cheeky introduction?

But if he had seen through OUR pretence of being ordinary shoppers, there was not much point in ignoring him, was there? And if he was setting a trap for us, it would be too late anyway. In that case he probably had accomplices close by who would see that we got no further than the exit of the station....

So I entered into his game and played a bogus aunt. With the help of the woman, I might discover, why he was on the road, and whether he truly needed our help.

"How is the family?" I asked, and got a short "O.K." as a reply, and then the woman joined in, wanting to know, why he had come to see us, even though it was term time?

He stuck his chin out and declared:

"Oh, lots of my mates have gone fruit picking, I thought I'd go as well!" He was no fool...it was, after all, September, and there were people helping with the apple and pear harvest everywhere. So this ruse deserved full marks!

But then he glanced to right and left, as if to make sure he wasn't being overheard, and asked:

"Do you want to know why I'm *really* here? The truth, I mean?"

"Yes, you'd better tell us." I said, trying to sound stern, at the same time studying his narrow frame. His clothing was tatty but clean, and his trousers, which were far too short for his skinny legs, showed new patches...so someone must care about his appearance! Even so, they looked as if they were about to fall apart at the catching of a bramble....

The boy whispered:

"I'm going to get Herrings!"

We stared at him, and the woman repeated:

"Herrings?"

"Yes, because I can swap two of them for a large loaf of bread; if you're lucky, you can even get some butter!"

All Because Of Him

"But how far have you got to go to get them?" I asked.

"Brunswick Market; some of my mates go once a fortnight."

We wanted to know what currency he could use, seeing that money from East Germany was useless in the West...and he told us that boys did errands for the traders, thus earning small amounts of cash, which in turn would pay for the fish....

"What do your parents think about it?" I asked, wondering how a mother could bear to let a child go on a trip like this! But he shrugged his bony shoulders and answered:

"Father got killed in Russia. I'm the eldest, I've got to help my mother feed us."

The woman said:

"But how can your mother bear to let you go?"

His eyes met hers, and he said sadly:

"She's not very well, and I've got two brothers and a sister, and they're always hungry; I've got to do SOMETHING!"

It was clear that he needed our help: He had such a hungerpinched face, and his over-large eyes were beseeching us when he said:

"This'll be my first trip, but I don't know the way."

There was nothing for it. We would have to take him. I turned to the woman for approval, and she nodded.

So it was agreed.

But three was enough.

More than three would look conspicuous, and we decided to make our departure there and then, before anyone else could approach us. The woman and I got up, straightened our clothes to give the impression that we weren't in any hurry, weren't rushing off for any speciasl reason. Everything had to appear as normal as possible, in case of any treacherous observers, even though by now the only people left in the waiting room, apart from ourselves were the old country men with their smelly pipes and their gossip.

All was well as we left the station, and with the boy walking between us, we took the road through the village, knowing that we were taking our first steps on a journey fraught with many perils. After a few minutes I glanced back:

We weren't being followed! The street behind us was empty.

"So far so good!" I said, and the boy remarked:

"They say three's a lucky number!"

The Applekeeper

He seemed relieved that he'd got over his first hurdle and found someone who knew the way. Apparently, his chums had told him about the path
we were to take, but he'd had no idea how to carry on after leaving the
village.

I thought he had lost a little of the pinched look, and now his expression
was more that of a boy setting out on an adventure....

But his observation about the lucky number three did nothing to cheer
up the woman. She said testily:

"That remains to be seen! We haven't crossed any bridges yet!"

I patted her arm:

"Remember the saying: The only thing to fear is fear!"

That was the moment I felt an invisible weight settle on my shoulders: It
was clear that from now on it would have to be me, who would answer for
the three of us!

Looking at two of them, it was plain to see that the woman would need
all her moral and physical strength, to keep going when we came to the
worst stretch of the journey.... And the boy was, after all, only a half-starved
kid. All I knew of him was that he was willing to take an enormous risk for
a few miserable pounds of salted fish!

Yet in spite of these misgivings, I was glad to have them as my travel
companions. And whatever happened, we were now all three tied to a common purpose. We would have to make the best of anything, whatever the
conditions.

So we kept on walking.

The landscape was dull and uninspirng. Nothing but fields for miles,
stretching across a plain literally as flat as a pancake. The only things taller
than the crops of cabbages, turnips and the bare stubbles of the harvested
grain were fruit trees. They were growing along the dry ditches on either
side of the road.

There are no hedges in the English sense in Germany, and apart from the
apple trees spreading their laden boughs to right and left above us, there
was no cover of any kind.

We appeared to be the only human beings amongst all that vegetation,
and as we were walking along, ripe apples were tempting us, beckoning
from above....

In areas such as this one, it used to be the custom to grow cherries,
plums, pears and apples by the roadsides; and to protect the harvest from

uninvited fruit pickers, villagers often clubbed together and employed an able-bodied pensioner to guard the trees. The job would fall to someone who would not mind spending his nights in the open, and was tough enough to take on any thieves.

Some of these elderly watchmen used to have a small shelter somewhere under the trees.

But at the time there was no keeper in sight, so we gave in to temptation and helped ourselves to a few ripe apples.

"What if anyone sees us?" The woman worried.

"Oh, the owners don't mind the odd few apples!" I said, "it's the organized plundering of the trees they have to guard against."

So we went on, munching and crunching, and no-one spoke until only the cores were left. I was hoping that my two companions were feeling as refreshed as I was: Even the endless, featureless plain seemed less dreary for a while....

"We should start looking for a shelter soon," I thought, "before it gets much later." Looking at the woman, I was sure she wouldn't take kindly to the idea of crouching in a ditch for several hours. I was still hoping to find something safer....

And as if she had read my thoughts, she began to fret:

"Is there no end to these fields? I can't see any place where we could rest!"

But the boy wasn't worried about a rest. He wanted to know why we couldn't just keep on walking, till we came to the forest?

"I'm not too tired, if you aren't!" He declared, and I was sure he meant it! But I had to disappoint him:

"It's no good getting anywhere near the forest until well after midnight!"

"Why not?"

"Because the Border Police *and* the Russian patrols will be out. The stretch past the barracks can't be done any other time."

The woman shuddered, and I said soothingly:

"Don't worry! We'll soon find a place!"

But her over-anxious mind was already leaping ahead to the next part of the trek. She wanted to know if I was sure to find my way in pitch darkness, especially when we had to spot the path into the forest....

I laughed and told her that I wasn't worried about the dark!

"They used to call me 'Cats'-Eyes' during the black-out! I've got excellent night-vision!"

"Oh, you make it sound so easy!" She said, and I went on as calmly as I could:

"You'll see: Once we've left the barracks behind, it'll be getting near dawn, and we'll find the opening among the undergrowth without much touble; as long as we get the timing right!"

In my own mind, however, I had to admit that her fears were well founded. I was not as sure of success as I tried to make out... but in contrast to her, I did not wish to dwell constantly on what might happen....

Of coursr it was true that the Police barracks with their dog kennels were going to pose a major obstacle! And to get past them unnoticed, even in the dark, depended on many things: There would have to be absolute silence, not even a whisper, no coughing, no stumbling or cracking of twigs.... I intended to brief her and the boy during our rest period, when we would decide on various hand signals we might use.

BUT: However careful we were in our movements, the main factor for our safety was beyond human control! The dirt track led along the side of some cabbage and clover fields, which would separate us from the barracks. They were large fields, surrounding the compound and stretching as far as the horizon: With the right wind we would stand a chance.

But if an eddying breeze were to reach the tracker dogs' noses, we wouldn't even make it past the first row of cabbages!

Still, all that was hours away yet, and for the moment the need to find a shelter was the main task. We continued walking, with everyone deep in their own thoughts and fears. I believe we each pictured a safe haven in our minds, as we continued to scan the landscape for a place to hide. In my case, I was imagining a cosy barn, full of sweet-smelling hay!

But I knew that there was no barn for miles around.

It looked as if it would have to be a clump of bushes growing from the ditch, a mean cover indeed, until about three a'clock in the morning!

The sun had gone down by now.

A dewy coolness was creeping out of the ground, touching our skin like clammy fingers; and I realized how wrong I'd been, to think the night would be fairly warm: We weren't in mid-summer!

It was a clear night in early September!

And being cold as well as feeling afraid, the woman now seemed in a worse plight than before. She jumped in terror as a harmless barn owl silently left its perch a little way ahead and floated away into the deepening dusk....

I sent up another of my quick 'Rocket Prayers', asking for her to have enough strength to last the course. Perhaps she had led a rather sheltered life up to now. I wondered how old she was? Perhaps not much older than myself, maybe in her mid-twenties...still, in a situation such as ours, it wasn't done to ask people's age, what did it matter, after all?

All we knew was that, for good or ill, we were bound together for a short space of time by a common need....

Formalities didn't come into it.

It struck me only much later, after it was all over, that none of us had even asked each other's name...and yet we had been as close as blood-brothers!

With the increasing dusk there came a sense of being adrift in an ocean of nothingness. The things which meant safety, warmth and comfort were lost somewhere far behind us....I remember thinking that wild animals must feel like this, when they try to flatten themselves against the ground, to become invisible to the hunters.

Still, we pressed on. No-one felt like talking. We were now so desperate for cover that even the luminous gold, which still clung to the sky in the West, could not rouse any comment of admiration. It didn't even dispel the glumness, when I pointed out the blue-black silhouette of the forest, where the sun had gone down.... All the woman said was:

"It seems such a long way off!"

Then the first star appeared and twinkled like a promise ahead of us. But twilight was gradually spreading its grey veil over everything, and with it an increasing gloom began to close in around our little group.

It felt as if we were being moved by forces outside our control, being led towards a goal which now seemed impossible to reach.

Then I remembered how, during the past few years, I'd had many dangerous situations to face. At times it had seemed as if I was no more than a leaf in a stream... being swept irresistably towards a weir some way ahead...but I'd always come through alright!

"It's time we shook ourselves out of this mood," I decided and whispered:

"Let's look on the bright side: When it gets too dark for us to see, it'll also be too dark for the patrols to spot us!"

The Applekeeper

But neither of them answered, it was now just a question of keeping going....

I don't remember who was the first one to spot the hut.

It was squatting under the trees some distance away and looked like a sort of small shelter.

We hesitated for a moment but then walked on, though our steps were getting slower and slower as we neared it.

I think all of us were asking the same silent question:

Whose hut was it? What if a Police patrol or even some Russians were hidden inside, just waiting to pounce?

But whoever might be concealed in it, it was too late to turn and run now. So we carefully advanced a little further, rather like Hansel and Gretel, when they came upon the witches' cottage... with hope and fear fighting for the upper hand.

Now we could make out that the door was slightly ajar.

We took the last few faltering steps towards it. I think we were all trying to fight back the panicky feeling somewhere inside us...and then we stopped dead:

Slowly, slowly, the door moved inwards on silent hinges.

It opened bit by bit, revealing a dark ominous whole, which held the three of us spellbound, while our eyes were trying to penetrate its blackness. I could neither speak nor swallow; my mouth was dry, and my tongue seemed glued to the roof of my mouth.

Then a shape appeared in the opening. It was an old man, gripping a stout knobstick.

He said nothing. He just stood there, his fist clutching his weapon, while his eyes were piercing the dusk, studying the trio in front of him.

I felt sure that even in this dim light he noticed everything: The two tired women with their stuffed holdalls and their stout walking shoes... the tattily clad youngster, who was facing him squarely, but was biting his lip like a school boy caught cheating, and I wondered if he could detect our feelings of despondency?

We stood rooted to the spot, like figures on a chess board, waiting for the next move...and when the old man broke the silence, he seemed to be muttering more to himself rather than addressing us...he said something about it being too early, about the Patrols being out until midnight, repeating several times: "No good yet... no good yet!"

All Because Of Him

What fools we'd been, to hope that anyone might take us for locals coming home from a shopping trip, when there was no dwelling anywhere in this vast emptiness of flat fields!

Of course, he had known the moment he saw us!

And he now appeared to be making up his mind about something. It was too dark to see his features clearly. The only thing plainly visible were his snow-white, bushy eyebrows: They were twitching like badgers' tails, while he was regarding our dejected looking little group....

So far, none of us had moved or spoken. We were waiting for his decision; and at last he said:

"Get in there! Looks bad if we stand outside, see?" He jerked his head towards the hut, and we obeyed, not yet certain whether it meant safety or if he was setting a trap: But what else could we do?

He followed us in and placed himself with his back against the door. He left it ajar, as we had first seen it, and, keeping his voice very low, he explained:

"Mustn't shut the door! Patrols look inside if it's shut!"

"DO they come past here?" The boy asked.

"Some nights they do... some nights they don't...damned if I know!"

He spoke in a kind of gruff whisper. His voice was not unkind, even though, to begin with, his short, chopped-off sentences were a little off-putting, and his last remarks put the woman into a new state of alarm! She wailed:

"So it isn't really safe in here,is it?"

"You never can tell," he said, "have them sit in here with me on rainy nights...other times they don't come out for days...wretched business! All of it!"

His answer did nothing to reassure her, but she said no more for the moment.

By now our eyes had got used to the dark interior , and we saw that a wooden bench ran along three sides of the hut. It was fixed to the walls and was the only comfort the place could boast of.

"Now," said our host, "sit behind the door, all three of you! Got a chance then... won't get seen!"

I hoped he was right and that if we sat as tightly packed as possible, no-one would   bother to look into our corner....

So we sat down, glad to have a rest. The only one still not at ease was the

...Of course he'd known the moment he saw us...

woman, who asked:

"But whose hut is this?"

"It's mine, see? Bought it after the war...been coming out here ever since...even when there's no apples."

I thought:

"So he is the local Applekeeper." And I wondered what had made him enter this dangerous game? Taking risks with the likes of us, instead of taking his ease at home, enjoying his retirement?

As if he'd guessed my thoughts, he said:

"It's peaceful out here, when there's nothing going on...and when there's trouble, I try'n do my bit."

"Peaceful," I thought, "that's a laugh! With all the Patrols, and people being shot at, or carted away to God knows where!"

Only much later did I, and the others, realize that there was a great deal more to his statement of 'doing his bit':

Apparently he had chosen to appear as just an old man who had taken on a rather thankless job. Being the local Applekeeper would deflect suspicion away from his real task, which was simply helping people get across to the West!

Like many a veteran from the first World War, he may have felt that he hadn't really 'done his bit' in the last conflict. Then he had seen a chance to be of use....

And he would probably keep at it till he was either found out or dropped dead in his tracks.

However, during that first part of the night, none of us thought of him as anything other than an old man, who happened to be there, when we needed him. And if we were lucky, he would help us to get to the other side.

We settled into the shadows behind the door, with our hold alls between our feet, ready to make a dash for it if need be, while the Applekeeper was giving us advice about the journey ahead....

He told us that he had grown up in these parts and knew our path well.

"Fair chance there," he said, "if you get the timing right!"

"Will you tell us when we should leave?" I asked him.

"Yea, I'll let you know! Got to get past the damn barracks while it's dark."

"What time should we leave then?" The boy put in, and the old man sniffed contemptuously:

The Applekeeper

"Don't know about that...don't go by them fancy watches...tell by the stars...much better!"

I felt sure he wouldn't let us down, but the woman still could not contain her fears:

"What if anyone comes and finds us in here?"

"Wait and see... just keep quiet and listen!"

He stepped outside, where he stood for a moment, sniffing, as if testing the night air. His silhouette was outlined darkly against the now star-bright sky.

There was no movement out there. The only sound was the hooting of an owl, somewhere across the fields.

"Must be off now," he muttered, "tons of apples...half of them left to rot...same as last year! Maybe people's too scared! Damned if I know!"

And having uttered what seemed to be his favourite phrase, he moved off. We stared after him in silence. Soon, the sound of his hob-nailed boots faded away in the distance.

It was pitch dark in the hut now, and no-one spoke.

The hard seat, which at first had been a welcome support, now made us shift our position every few minutes. Leaning against the wall one moment and slumping forward the next, we tried in vain to find some comfort. There was little hope of getting any sleep for the time being. We were far too tense.

About an hour later, we heard steps....

They were coming closer. Then came the sound of someone talking in undertones...and we gripped our bags, ready to burst from the hut! But then we recognized the voice of the Applekeeper...and soon we could make out what he was saying:

"Must ask them first,see? Can't spring it on them...too risky! Maybe they will...an' maybe they won't. Damned if I know!"

Now the black shape of the old man appeared in the doorway. He cleared his throat, shuffled his feet, jerked his head towards the night outside and said hoarsely:

"Got a man out there, says he's escaped from the Uranium Mines in Silesia! Says he's got to get away fast! Bloke showed him the way from the station... now he's lost...see?"

We saw alright!

AND we knew what this might mean!

All Because Of Him

It was very still in our hide-out for what felt like eternity. It was an utterly selfish silence, and it must have weighed heavily on the quiet figure waiting by the wayside.

I thought he must feel like a prisoner awaiting his verdict. His silent plea seemed to fill the air....

But what about our resolution that there should be no more than the three of us?

And there would be a much greater risk for us all!

All these thoughts were going through my head, and I knew from the way my companions were shifting uneasily, and breathing as if they were literally being pressed by something, that they must be thinking on the same lines....

Then I broke the terrible silence and asked:

"Has he got any papers on him?"

"Only Labour-Camp-Card!" The old man gruffed, "an'you know what *that* means! If you get caught, it'll be SIBERIA...not Silesia for *him*!"

I believe that was the moment the woman, the boy and I felt our resolve crumble. The superstition about the lucky number three was being swept away by the stranger's need for our help.

When we talked about it later, we all said that, deep inside us, there rose the certain knowledge that if we were to refuse, none of us would make it to the other side either! Somehow, our selfishness would summon up all the powers of evil to array themselves against us!

And so it was settled.

Looking back it seems strange that we came to the decision without any more words....

Even the woman agreed with just a deep sigh of acceptance.

"Tell him to come inside." I whispered, "and tell him he'd better swallow his Labour-Camp-Card, if we run into trouble!"

The Applekeeper turned to the man outside, while the three of us wriggled still further into our corner behind the door, making room for the newcomer.

"Go on in," we heard the old man say,"and remember: NO noise!"

We heard him clip-clopping away, and then the stranger slipped in quietly.

"God bless you for this!" He murmured and collapsed onto the seat opposite us. It was too dark to see his features, all we could discern was a human form of, perhaps, medium height.

He took off his rucksack.

We could tell by the way it dropped to the ground, with a sort of weightless flop, that its owner was probably at the end of his resources, in every sense of the word. I wondered when he had last eaten, but it might be best to let him sit quietly for a few minutes....

When he appeared to have got his breath back, we explained to him that he would have to sit on our side of the bench, because of the open door.

He came across and sat between us two women, with the lad pressed into the very corner at the end of the seat. It was a tight squeeze, but at least it kept us warm during those seemingly endless hours of waiting.

The newcomer seemed to feel that he owed us an explanation. He started to talk about his escape, but his voice, coming in short gasps, betrayed his exhaustion. Apparently he hadn't eaten since the morning of the previous day, but when we offered him some of our food, he said he was too tired even to feel hungry....

So we let him be, and soon the intervals between his hoarsely whispered utterances became longer and longer, until, finally, sleep got the better of him. And he slept like a log....

After a while, he seemed to be slipping of his seat, and the woman and I raised him as best we could without waking him. Then we took turns in bedding his head against our shoulders.

The boy, too, kept dozing off every now and then, while the woman and I were listening to the night noises, waiting for time to tick itself out, and for the morning to draw nearer.

All was quiet outside.

About midnight she whispered:

"You know what strikes me as funny?"

"No." I whispered back.

"Neither you nor I asked any questions WHY we are going across; we just trusted each other from the start!"

"That's all that's needed, anyway."

It was meant to sound reassuring, but at the same time I didn't feel I wanted to discuss my own reasons with a stranger.

I was far too miserable about the final break-up of my marriage and about my husband's refusal to listen to reason. He was an only son who had been rather spoiled; and he had believed the lies his mother had told him....

All Because Of Him

Looking back to the first few months after the war, I thought sadly of the time I had spent with Karl's aunt and uncle. I used to lie awake at night listening for his footsteps, praying that he would return from wherever he'd been taken prisoner! And during all that time I'd had no idea of the rumours the village people had spread.... Even now it seemed too absurd for words! But I had been so ignorant of human malice!

It had'nt occurred to me that the neighbours of Karl's aunt, watching from behind curtains, were drawing the wrong conclusions and were making it their business to scatter the news!

It had all started, with Janush, the Polish prisoner working at the farm....

Janush was well respected by the aunt, and grudgingly accepted by the uncle. The latter had to admit that he couldn't have done without the Pole's help, seeing that his own son was somewhere at the front. The aunt had even insisted that Janush should have his meals with them in the kitchen, not in the barn like the prisoners on other farms!

I had been staying there since the end of March, after we lost our flat. I hadn't really got to know the young Pole. But I thought he seemed upright and honest and was probably in his late twenties.

Then one morning I had taken advantage of the aunt's absence and was listening to the BBC, when Janush walked in from the yard!

Now we both knew that listening to a foreign radio station was classed as treason; and for a moment I felt afraid!

He seemed to realize at once what I was doing; but to my relief his usually serious face lit up in a beaming smile. He came across the kitchen, held out his hand and said:

"Now we be friends! I trust you...you trust me!"

So we shook hands on it....

And since that day, there was a sort of bond between us: He had a German girl friend, a farmer's daughter in the next village... and though his spoken German was good, he felt lost, when it came to writing a love letter!

One day he asked me to write a note to the young woman, and we agreed that we would meet in the barn after the day's work. We thought no-one would see us there, because it was a crime to 'consort' with a P.O.W!

But, of course, when I was writing his messages, I hadn't reckoned with the curtain twitchers, who were watching the barn doors from their lookouts opposite!

For Janush and me, it had been the most natural thing to help each other... but not for those neighbours!

Oh, I must have been so blind!

During the days the Americans took over the area, I had been visiting some cousins in the neighbourhood, and when I returned to aunt Minnie's place, I found Janush was still working there, even though he was now free.

He told me that he was hoping to remain in Germany, marry his German girl and settle down....

And now it got worse, as far as the curtain twitchers were concerned:

I was helping with the work in the fields, hoeing, cutting thistles, collecting baskets and baskets full of stones from the soil....(It was long before the days of mechanisation!) And as the hot sun used to give me splitting headaches, I asked the aunt, if I could go out before it got hot and do my share then.

But she didn't think it would be safe to be out by myself, because after the Allies had moved into the villages, the country roads were swamped with people from everywhere, trying to return to their homes, trying to find lost relatives, or attempting to hide from the arms of the law....

It was hard to tell who was who.

So Janush had offered to come with me, and she had agreed, had even ignored the uncle's grumbles about 'gadding about before the crack of dawn'!

We had enjoyed the cool mornings, had watched the hares playing in the corn, and had listened to the larks while we were working.

I had got on twice as fast, because it was pleasant not to be out in the burning heat. Janush had insisted I shouldn't carry the baskets full of stones from one end of the field to the other, and we'd worked out a scheme by which we both did the collecting, but he did all the carrying.

All had been well, till the uncle said one morning:

"You're not going with that Pole any more, people are talking!"

I hadn't expected this and asked:

"About what?"

"You, of course! You, carrying on with that damn prisoner!"

"But he is no longer a prisoner!" I retorted angrily. "He's working for you of his own free will! And as for talking: There's nothing to talk about!"

But it was no use.

The aunt now chimed in, saying that her husband was right, and I should

All Because Of Him

have to go out to the fields with the team of women.

So we had to stop our early mornings together, and I felt sad about it. On the way to the fields, we had been telling each other of our hopes and dreams: Janush talked of marrying his German girl, and I had told him of the happy days during the first years of our marriage.

When, on several occasions, I had voiced my fears about Karl's safe return and about his parents' antagonism towards me, Janus had tried to reassure me, had told me that there were many thousands of German prisoners still waiting to be released....

And on the subject of Karl's parents he used to laugh and say:

"He'll come back to YOU! You'll see! He not want to live without YOU!"

But he had been wrong....

I had given up the contest, and now, sitting in the old Apple- keepers hut, I was about to leave all those shattered dreams behind. It had taken three years of struggling , of trying to win Karl back from the effects of Mother-in-law's poisonous tongue. She had lapped up the gossip about Janush and me and couldn't wait to tell her son about it!

In the time since he'd been released from the prison camp, he had not once let me explain how the rumours had come about. He had refused to discuss it; and in the end, his mother had won!

But it was no use dwelling on it now. For the moment all that mattered was to get away safely.

We had been sitting in silence for a while, but it seemed that the woman now seemed to feel a need to talk, maybe to relieve the tension, and so she whispered:

"Would you mind, if I told you why I'm going?"

"If you really want to," I answered, not wishing to sound uncaring and remembering how I had wondered earlier on, why she was making the trip....

She seemed such a quiet, unassuming person, and I'd learnt already that she was easily scared, so why was she here?

But listening to her, I began to see her in a different light. I even had to admire her, in spite of all the worrying and fretting during the past few hours!

It seemed that the trek was more like a kind of pilgrimage, as far as she was concerned....

She and her husband lived in one of the more fashionable areas of

The Applekeeper

Magdeburg. Her neighbourhood had suffered very little bomb damage; so they still had their comfortable, well furnished house,and her husband still had a flourishing business....

So it seemed they really lacked nothing!

"Except we can't have children," she said sadly, and then went on to tell me that she was on the way to her sister, who lived in Hamburg. The sister was going to pay for an operation which might give her a chance to have a baby.

"You see, the clinics in the Russian Sector haven't got the facilities; so I have to go."

She sighed deeply, and I sat quietly...what could I say?

I did not ask her why she had not applied for an official pass: She was young and of 'working age', so she wouldn't have got one in any case! Nor did it surprise me that her husband was letting her make the trip on her own. He would only have increased the risk during the crossing; and if they'd been discovered, he would have lost his business, maybe even his freedom.

So here she was, afraid as a mouse in a trap, yet willing to risk life and limb for the chance of fulfilling a dream....And all I could do was hope that eventually there would be an answer to her prayers....

Sitting in silence again, with the fugitive's head pressing on my shoulder, I thought how, in one way or another, all four of us were on the run, even though for very different reasons:

We were all trying to escape from a life which had become intolerable or meaningless: Even the boy, who had chosen to take up smuggling rather than face the daily misery of watching his family starve....

If we succeeded, the woman and the boy would go back, though the man and I would never return. Once we reached the West, he would be free, free to begin a new life; and I, too, would make a fresh start, IF we got through the next few hours safely!

Oh, the night seemed to be full of 'IFs'!

It was well past midnight, when we heard voices in the distance, but they died away, and after a few minutes of intense listening, we heard the shuffling steps of the Applekeeper.

He was alone when he pushed open the door and told us:

"All gone quiet now! Russians gone away to a boozing party ... and Police turned in for the night!"

I suddenly realized he hadn't been whispering but had talked normally!

So it must be safe now. But again, the anxious woman had to be reassured:

"How do you know about the Russians?"

He told us that he'd heard it from one of the Policemen out on patrol:

"Quite a decent sort of bloke, that one... how he ever joined that blasted mob...I'm damned if I know!"

He sniffed, or rather snorted contemptuously at the thought of the hated Border Police, and then went on:

"Is all right if you want to stretch your legs outside a bit. Or if you want to sleep...I'll wake you when it's time."

And off he trotted into the night once again.

For the moment we remained in our cramped positions, because we wanted to let the man go on sleeping, and during the next half hour or so, we tried in vain to get some sleep ourselves. With legs aching, backs and shoulders stiff and sore, our heads felt like separate parts, nodding about on top of our necks....

When I tried for the umpteenth time to find a more tolerable position, the man on my shoulder awoke.

He gave a start, sat bolt-upright, then remembered where he was and appeared to relax... after a long shuddering sigh of relief, he said slowly:

"Are you sure you want to take me with you? You can still change your mind, you know! It's a big risk taking me!"

But by now there was no question of reconsidering. Now we were able to talk freely, the mood seemed to have changed, and we felt ready for almost anything!

First of all, though, we followed the Applekeeper's advice to 'stretch our legs for a minute'... which meant in real terms that we took it in turns to follow the call of nature. And after we had all taken the air, we settled ourselves a little more comfortably, now that we could use all parts of the seat. The woman and I remained behind the door, while the man and the boy took the side near the opening.

"Cor!" murmued the boy, "I've never felt so grateful in all my life to be allowed to go behind a bush!"

He had spoken for us all. And now that we'd felt the coolness of the night air outside, the little cabin felt almost cosy, and we pushed the door as near shut as we dared to keep out the clamminess.

The woman suggested that now was the time to have something to eat....

It was a strange feast.

The Applekeeper

She and I spread out our sandwiches on a piece of grease-proof paper on the floor. The youngster fished a pitifully small parcel from his rucksack and placed it next to our pile. He'd only been given two rounds of bread, scraped with dripping...I supposed it was all his mother could spare.

Then the man was grappling with his rucksack, trying to undo the drawstring. It was too dark to see the lump of dry bread he retrieved from its depth, and he said apologetically:

"I've only got this crust, saved it for the last lap. Sorry I can't offer you anything else."

The woman and I felt very small and refused to take his Iron Ration, insisting that we all shared the sandwiches.

Neither of us women had suffered hunger the way the boy and the fugitive had done, so she and I ate slowly... leaving the lion's share to the men. It was good to hear them eat, sensing their pleasure, even though we couldn't see their faces....

After a while, when nothing was left but the grease-proof paper, the woman took a flask from her hold-all. We heard her remove the cork and pour something into a mug.

And lo and behold! The near-forgotten smell of *real* coffee started wafting through the hut, creeping up our nostrils, waking memories of better days....

"Here you are, you need it most," she said, reaching out in the darkness to where the fugitive was sitting. He took the mug from her so reverently, it might have been the Holy Grail!

And he sipped the precious liquid slowly, savouring it to the very last drop. Then we each in turn received our share. What a treat! Apart from the woman, none of us had tasted real coffee for years.... She told us that she had made it extra strong to fight fatigue; and that was exactly what it had done for all of us!

The delicious brew revived our spirits and loosened our tongues. Even the spartan comforts of our hide-out suddenly seemed less wooden and cramped!

After that, we spent the rest of the small hours discussing details of the route... and what to do in case of approaching trouble....

Finally, in an attempt at light-heartedness, we ended up telling stories and jokes, until, about half past three, the Applekeeper arrived and told us it was time to go.

All Because Of Him

We got up to be on our way, somehow a little lost for the right words now that it was time to leave....

The boy asked the old man, why he had not come and sat with us?

"After all," he said, "it's *your* hut! So why did you stay out all night?"

The Applekeeper cleared his throat, and though we could not see his face, I thought he was probably smiling, as if he was pleased with something he'd acchieved:

"Ah, that would've looked bad, see?"

"Why?" We all wanted to know.

"I never knew you was in my hut...see? No never! If they catch me... talking to folks like you...would be the end of this here job!"

I felt he really was one of the unsung heros of our time, and yet he made it all sound quite simple. I asked:

"But doesn't anyone suspect what you are doing?"

I couldn't see his grin...but I'm sure it was there, when he said:

"Got be be smart: Pretend I'm a bit slow... they think I'm a half-witted old fogey!"

The woman breathed a sort of sigh of admiration:

"I think that's incredible! The risks you are taking!"

"So what?" He asked, and then, falling back into his gruff way of talking, he went on:

"Got to keep going...got to do my bit for them that's on the run...don't know for how long...damned if I know!"

"Is the path still used a lot?" The boy asked, and the old man said:

"Oh, there's not many come past here these days," he said. "It's getting too tricky...lots of shooting around here a night or two ago...."

He stopped on a quick intake of breath. Maybe he had realized that this was not the time to talk about shooting, when there was no chance of turning back, and I found myself wishing he hadn't made that last remark!

Still, we were indebted to him:

He had given up his resting place to shelter us. When he had first asked us in, he had not even hinted that it would mean a night out in the open for him.

It was time to go, though, and we all shook hands. Then, as we were about to leave the hut, the old man produced four apples from his knapsack and handed one to each of us.

"Best coxes," he said, "not supposed to pick them...but they's for luck!"

The Applekeeper

We thanked him for everything, pocketed the apples and stepped outside, leaving him standing in the doorway. I felt sure he remained there, listening to the sound of our footsteps, till they'd died away....

Once more we were on the cobbled road, on the last and most hazardous part of our journey.

We reckoned to be able to do the first stretch, as far as the barracks, in about half an hour or so; and soon after we had passed them, we would have to turn off into a farm track, where we should have to proceed in single file.

I had explained the need for this after our meal in the hut, so we all knew what to do, and for the moment we just pressed on, walking very fast to get over this first major hurdle.

Soon we saw a cluster of low buildings looming some way ahead on our right....

There it was: The Police Compound!

It was only just discernible as a darker shade of the darkness around it. But to us it looked menacing, like a cowering monster, ready to spring, ready to undo all our hopes and plans if we gave it an inkling of our presence.

We'd been walking so fast, and now we felt even the sound of our breath might give us away!

I spat on my right forefinger and held it above my head: A faint breeze was blowing towards us from the place of peril....That was a relief! All was well so far... our scent would not be carried to the kennels. The man-hunting dogs could sleep on.

At the pace we were moving, it did not take long to leave the threatening shadows behind us. And when I looked back after half a mile or so, the first pale glimmer of light appeared behind us in the East... I whispered to the woman:

"We'll make the woods in good time!"

By the time we reached the beginning of the mud track the stars were disappearing one by one.

We stopped for a moment.

Walking along this track, which was just wide enough to admit a tractor, we would be covered on our left by clumps of hazel, bramble and bracken and a few small trees, but on our right there would only be cabbage and clover fields...nothing high enough to hide in! But beyond those fields and straight ahead of us there arose the outline of the great forest!

All Because Of Him

We now arranged ourselves in the order we'd decided on while we were still in the Applekeeper's hut:

From here on, the man was to walk behind me, followed by the woman and the boy. Should anyone approach from in front or from the rear, the man was to drop to the ground and crawl into the bushes on the left, while the two who were following him were to step over him and keep going...we were hoping thus to try and cover his escape.

After we'd nodded at each other, sort of O.K.-ing the manoeuvre, we started walking again. Even though we had passed the Police Barracks, we would still communicate only by sign language as much as possible.

The path was deeply rutted from the tyres of some farm vehicle. The ruts were hardened and sun-baked, probably made several days ago, when we'd had rain....

Suddenly the boy whispered:

"Look! Tyre marks of a motorbike...on top of the tractor ones."

"Police?" The woman breathed, pressing her hand to her mouth.

The man examined the imprints....

"No, the motorbike marks aren't fresh! See where it skidded on that cow pat? It's had at least a couple of days' drying in the sun!"

I prayed that he was right, but I wasn't easy in my mind about those tyre marks.... Whoever would think of escaping on a noisy thing like a motor bike?

But if the others felt the same, no-one remarked on it, as we stumbled more than walked along the uneven ruts.

Ahead of us we could now see more and more of the shadowy outline of the forest. It still had no form, except that of a dark wall in a world of luminous grey....

We were passing the broad fields with nothing but cabbages. In the dim light they looked like heads stuck on poles...and I told myself to keep going and not to imagine things!

At the first sign of real light, when our surroundings were beginning to take on colours, we reached the clover fields...an endless sea of green.

An owl took off from the thicket on our left, only a stone's throw away; and a few steps further on, a rabbit hobbled out from under a bush. It crossed our path and disappeared in the deep clover.

"Very good signs!" The man whispered. "No living soul's about apart from us!"

The Applekeeper

"How come?" Whispered the boy.

"Because if there was, those animals wouldn't be here! It was *us* that startled them!"

Silence again.

There were more and more trees on our left now, like a sort of 'outposts' of the forest. We were getting ever closer and could see the tips of the trees ahead, shining pink and golden in the early morning light. Very soon, we would be able to spy the dark entrance to our path in amongst the undergrowth....

And then I saw the motorbike!

It was lying on its side in the clover...glistening with dew...and it looked abandoned and sinister....

As I stopped short, the man behind me dropped noiselessly to the ground, but the woman put her hand on his shoulder and pointed to the number plate, which had neither Russian nor Police markings: It was quite obviously a civilian machine.

So he got to his feet again, and we continued, again without speaking... but by now each of us was feeling the tension mounting with every step we took....

Then there was a sudden buzzing of flies, horrid big things that feed on offal... they swarmed up from a patch in the clover close to the edge of the field....

And there, a few feet away from the track, was the man who had owned the motorbike!

He was lying quite still, half buried in the fresh green, and as we neared him, more flies were rising from his blood encrusted hair.... He had been shot through the head!

For one fearful moment I thought the woman was going to faint! She was swaying on her feet, and I gripped her arm and hissed with as much firmness as I could muster:

"Keep going! We can't help him! He's dead! Keep walking!"

Once again I thanked fate for that inner calmness that always used to get hold of me in an emergency! I couldn't count the times it had saved me before...and it didn't let me down now.

After we'd passed the dead man, I let go of her arm, took her by the hand and guided her along the path, promising:

"Only a few more steps! Look, there's the opening under the trees! We mustn't give up now!"

By the time we entered the forest, she had recovered enough to walk unaided. We were still walking in single file. The path was narrow, but not as overgrown as I had feared.

From above us, the unmelodious cry of a jay tore the silence. It left its perch, annoyed at our intrusion. The man had been right, when he said that we were the only living souls in the area:

The dew in the grass at our feet lay sparkling and undisturbed.

It was pleasant to walk on the soft green carpet after the rough going on the farm track. The light shining through the branches of the forest canopy was golden-green...so the sun must be up at last! It would soon be hot out there in the clover....

It seemed everyone's thoughts were with the dead man, and none of us felt like talking for a long time.

Then the fugitive said:

"Poor devil! So close, and he never made it!"

Silence again....

The path had broadened out after the first mile or so. We were moving as fast as we could, but no longer in single file. The man was breathing heavily, and the woman was making quick jerky steps to keep up with our desperate pace.

Only the lad, who was now walking by my side, appeared able to match my stride without faltering.

I thought we must be nearing the border, when we came to a new obstacle, and once more we held our breath in fear of the unknown:

In front of us, right across our path there was a huge bank of earth! On my last trip a few months ago, when I had gone to visit my parents in Hanover, this had not been here!

It was obvious that the authorities were tightening the net all over the place. (Even though, as I mentioned earlier, at that time there were no barbed wires, mine fields and watch towers in that area yet.)

What should we do?

Behind that bank there would be a ditch deep enough to hide the guards...they could pick off the travellers one by one, as if they were targets in a shooting gallery at a fair ground!

We stopped and listened, waiting to see if anything moved on the far side of the mound of earth....

The Applekeeper

But then, if the ditch *was* manned, it was useless to try and out-manoeuver the snipers. It would be no good turning back and scrambling through the bushes somewhere by the side of the path...and while we were still whispering about a way out or around or over it, a heaven-sent blackbird made up our minds for us:

It flew out of a bush on the very edge of the bank, chattering angrily! It told us we were safe, and we blessed its presence there....

One after the other, we scrambled up over the loose soil, jumped the ditch on the other side and sped on again.

We were now on the very last lap of our trek.

Not much further, and we could see the official sign-post through the trees, telling us that we were now entering the British Zone!

The first one to pass the spot was the fugitive....

He must have gone through agonies during the last few hours! Sweat was running down his face, and the veins on his temples and neck were throbbing!

And now, still within sight of the sign-post, he suddenly declared that he could go no further, and with that he sat down heavily on the nearest tree trunk!

But the woman and I gripped him firmly by his arms and pulled him along to where we should be safer.

It was hard to explain to the exhausted man that we could not relax till we were within sight and sound of the Autobahn....

Because in these very woods some run-aways had been hauled back from well within the British Sector!

"O.K.," he sighed, and followed us to where we could hear the roar of big engines on the Dual-carriage way. Soon we came to a clearing, and through the trees we could see Army-lorries rolling by: They bore the British insignias....

We had made it!

The clearing was like a huge mossy cushion, just the place to have a rest and relax for a while. So I stopped and said:

"You are safe now!"

And even though he was years older than any of us, he snatched off his crumpled old hat, threw it high into the green dome above us and let out a wild shout of joy!

Then he flung himself down on the deep moss and buried his face in the healing coolness of it....

He was free!

No need to run any more....

The woman, the boy and I sat down a little way off and waited. We could see his shoulders heaving...he was sobbing with relief.

When he had calmed down, the woman said:

"Let's eat our apples now, shall we? As a sort of toast to the old Applekeeper."

"Yes, let's!" the boy agreed, and the fugitive added:

"Where would we have been without him? See what a risk he took!"

"So here's to the Applekeeper!" I said, and we ate his apples. By the time we'd finished, we all seemed ready for the next stage of the journey... and the man cleared his throat and said he wanted to thank all three of us for helping him across!

But we stopped him.

We remembered our reluctance during the night, when we hadn't wanted to take on a fourth member! We didn't feel we deserved any praise....

"All right," he said, "let's say good-bye then. And I'll tell you what I'll do."

He jumped to his feet and took both my hands in his; then he said in a voice charged with emotion:

"I'll go and find a horse in a field somewhere, and I'll give him my last piece of bread as a thank-offering."